IN PURSUIT OF UNHAPPINESS

IN PURSUIT OF UNHAPPINESS

Reflections on Suicide

RAMIN JAHANBEGLOO

Orient BlackSwan

IN PURSUIT OF UNHAPPINESS: REFLECTIONS ON SUICIDE

ORIENT BLACKSWAN PRIVATE LIMITED

Registered Office
3-6-752 Himayatnagar, Hyderabad 500 029, Telangana, India
e-mail: centraloffice@orientblackswan.com

Other Offices
Bengaluru, Chennai, Guwahati, Hyderabad,
Kolkata, Lucknow, Mumbai, New Delhi,
Noida, Patna, Visakhapatnam

First published by Orient Blackswan Private Limited 2021

ISBN 978-81-948295-7-7

032534

Typeset in
Constantia 10.5/13
by Le Studio Graphique, Gurgaon 122 007

Printed in India at
Akash Press, New Delhi 110020

Published by
Orient Blackswan Private Limited
3-6-752 Himayatnagar, Hyderabad 500 029, Telangana, India
e-mail: info@orientblackswan.com

In memory of Hossein Ziai,
Professor at UCLA,
who preferred death to indignity

CONTENTS

1 INTRODUCTION

Why Suicide?

Albert Camus famously wrote: 'There is but one truly serious philosophical problem and that is suicide' (Camus 1975: 1). However, in trying to address this problem, Camus was emphasising, over and above everything else, the value of life. If it is true that life is worth living, then why is it that when life ceases to be worthwhile, putting an end to one's misery, suffering and despair by ending one's life is still considered by our decivilising society to be a criminal act rather than a philosophical problem? People are still bewildered, unnerved and devastated by the suicides of writers, artists and philosophers, while they remain disturbingly unaware of and misguided as to the reasons behind such acts. The act of suicide is still seen by society as something intolerable, unacceptable and, for the most part, a public and mental health issue, rather than a genuine philosophical question to be understood and debated. We continue to view suicide as an individual's extreme contempt for life and as an outrage to humanity (as Kant formulates it). But suicide is neither of these; it represents the highest form of human freedom—the freedom *not to be*. More than just an attitude towards self-destruction, suicide is the last temptation towards human self-affirmation. But this self-affirmation, which is accompanied by a consciousness of freedom, is expressed in the form of anguish. Jean Paul Sartre uses the metaphor of a man standing on the edge of a cliff and experiencing the dizziness of a compelling need, an overpowering urge to answer the call of the void. This is one of the most significant sections in *Being and Nothingness*, where Sartre describes this moment of vertigo as the fragility of human freedom. According to Sartre, at that particular moment, the individual has the freedom to choose—to jump off the cliff and die, or to move back to safety and life. The freedom of having a choice between being and not being creates a peculiar and intense anguish. As Sartre acutely and brilliantly describes,

> Vertigo announces itself through fear; I am on a narrow path—without a guardrail—which goes along a precipice. The precipice...represents a danger of death. At the same time, I conceive of...causes... which can transform that threat of death into reality; I can slip on a stone and fall into the abyss...I am passive in relation to these possibilities...At this moment *fear* appears, which...is the apprehension of myself as a destructible transcendent in the midst of transcendents...My reaction will be [to]...keep myself as far as possible from the edge...as repudiating the threatening situation with all my strength...These actions are *my* possibilities. (Sartre 1956: 30)

It is by projecting such possible future human action and *agency* against the imminent threat of death and its *passive* acceptance that the individual can escape fear, and reclaim authorship of life and death. Following Sartre, one can say that suicide is possible because human beings are conscious of their freedom. This consciousness is the primary locus of the anguish in front of the fear of absolute freedom and the nothingness of death. Anguish is not fear. Anguish is a possibility—suicide is a possible course of action and a choice in front of us. That is where the anguish comes from: we are afraid of what we can do; we are afraid of our absolute freedom. Therefore, it would be wrong to consider suicide a gratuitous act. Suicide is not the absence or the flip side of freedom, but an affirmation of freedom as the negation of being. The gesture of ending one's own life only makes sense in an existence that is aware of itself. Unlike death, suicide is an experience to which we can appeal and relate. Unlike natural death, every suicide is unique and irreplaceable. Man has the choice not to kill himself. Therefore, like other life experiences, one could say that suicide, too, is an experience that gives meaning to life; it is a journey towards shaping human destiny.

The notion of suicide is as old as human civilisation. According to Alfred Alvarez, possibly the earliest mention of the word *suicide* as we use it today was in the *Religio Medici* of Sir Thomas Browne in 1635 AD. 'The primitive horror of suicide, which survived so long in Europe, was then a horror of blood evilly spilt and unappeased. In practice, this meant that suicide was equated with murder' (Alvarez 1971: 68). The ancient Greeks, however, looked at the idea of 'self-killing' somewhat differently.

> In classical Greece, philosophical discussions of suicide were dictated by calm reasonableness. In ancient Athens, the magistrates kept a supply of hemlock on hand for those who wished to end their lives. Official permission for use of the poison had to be obtained from the Senate however, for the private act of suicide was under public jurisdiction...only if a life was officially decreed *immoderate*, and therefore *intolerable*, that suicide could be legally committed. The state not only had the right to allow or deny a lethal dosage of hemlock, it could also prescribe it as a form of capital punishment. (Noon 1978: 372–373; emphases added)

Even so, suicide was not encouraged by law in classical Greece. Athenian law condemned suicide as illegal because the Athenians believed that suicide was harmful to the *polis*, and not to the individual. Aristotle discusses this at the end of the fifth book of *The Nicomachean Ethics*. According to him:

> the law does not order a man to kill himself; and what the law does not order it forbids...the man who kills himself in a rage voluntarily acts thus against right reason and does what the law forbids: he acts unjustly therefore. But unjustly to whom? To the state surely, not to himself; for he suffers voluntarily, but no one can have an injustice done him voluntarily. And upon this ground the state actually punishes him, i.e. it pronounces a particular kind of disfranchisement upon the man who destroys himself, as one who acts unjustly towards the state. (Aristotle 1884: 177)

Clearly, what Aristotle is referring to above is the necessity of a moral code based on utilitarian observances of the Athenian polis. In other words, the Athenians distinguished plainly between self-sacrifice for the city-state and suicide as self-murder. As Elise P. Garrison elaborates, Thucydides, while recounting the tragic Corcyraean civil war episode of the Peloponnesian War, the 'anomic state of affairs at Corcyra' and 'the general chaos and despair that accompanies revolution', also mentions 'the suicide of the Messenian prisoners who refused to be tried by their captors' (Garrison 1991: 13–14). Garrison goes on to note that,

> Usually, neither Thucydides nor Herodotus makes any explicit value judgments concerning the suicide victims they mention, but implicitly, by using an evocative word, by creating a tragic atmosphere, by imputing the same motivations to Greeks and barbarians alike, and by conceding—or rather, by the very act of recording the events without blame, helping

> to create—pity and honor for many of the victims, they leave us with the sense that suicide created no 'moral revulsion,' but rather provided people with an honorable release from an undesirable life, a life made unbearable because of shame or dishonor, i.e., because of unfavorable societal perception. (Garrison 1991: 13–14)

This sense of shame is a recurrent theme in Greek tragedies, where suicide is the result of a social failure by the individual. It is invariably the weight of social pressure which drives the protagonist to suicide. In this matter, Sophocles was undoubtedly the godfather, for in six of his seven plays there is at least one suicide or threat to suicide: 'Ajax, Antigone, Eurydice, Haemon, Deianeira and Jocasta all kill themselves, while Electra and Philoctetes threaten to do so, and the chorus fears Oedipus may kill himself. All of the suicides Sophocles depicts as noble and understandable, and all of the victims kill themselves in response to societal pressures' (Garrison 1991: 21). Among all these, Antigone's suicide has stayed with us, not as a manifestation of despair, but as an expression of revolt and disobedience. In a very existential manner, Antigone takes control of her destiny by hanging herself with her girdle. Antigone's choice to confront death by suicide is her way of honouring the Athenian polis, while at the same time disobeying the king, Creon. For her, suicide is a political act which honours the death of her brother Polynices and mourns him, in open defiance of Creon's edict that he shall remain unmourned. Antigone sees her suicide as an honourable death which will dignify the public memory of her family. Significantly, Antigone's suicide also takes place in an ethical framework, within which she sees herself as someone taking a stance and making a larger moral statement, which goes beyond her as an individual and her act of self-killing. In her embracement of this ethical framework, Antigone's tragic suicide and her disobedience of the king are also acts of self-affirmation, which clearly point to a direct connection between suicide and revolt.

As such, whenever we talk about suicide, we really mean being a spectator to one's own death. But it is also at the same time, as Camus says, a re-evaluation of one's life. The value of our life depends on the intent, the dignity and the clarity with which we live it, among other things. The value of a life also determines the value of its death. Therefore, not all suicides are equal and not all are worthwhile. Some suicides are not worthwhile even for the person who commits suicide. However, among the more famous suicides in human history and literature, there are some which have been deemed praiseworthy, as exemplary moral, political and/or aesthetic attitudes toward life and death, and others which have been condemned because of their meaninglessness. Whether in forms of tragic narratives or in real-life experiences, suicides of fictional and historical figures like Antigone, Socrates, Gerard de Nerval, Virginia Woolf, Vladimir Mayakovsky, Walter Benjamin, Sadeq Hedayat and Yukio Mishima stand out as a protest against the mediocrity and meaninglessness of their times. Or perhaps, this is what happens when a beautiful mind encounters the ugliness and banality of others. Truly, it is in their suicides that these creators of art and animators of ideas found the real meaning of their lives. As Shakespeare says in *Richard II* (Act III, Scene 2, line 152): 'Nothing can we call our own but death' (Shakespeare 1770: 43). Death is something that we apprehend from the outside, while suicide is something which is experienced from the inside. It is true that with the rise of individual agency as a Cartesian subject and personal autonomy in early modern art and philosophy, a new door of perception opened to the problem of suicide. The ultimate negation of the subject in the act of suicide went hand in hand with the self-assertion of the same subject as a self-conscious individual. Few have shown more powerfully, or with greater irony, this heroic struggle between the individual life-affirming quest for self and the profound psychological temptation to self-destruct than Shakespeare.

If death in general and suicide in particular are brought into discussion in the dramatic expression of Shakespeare, it is mainly due to the fact that suicidal messages tend to have a communicative quality. According to Eric Langley,

> early modern drama incorporates suicide as an integral aspect of its broader consideration of humanist self-determination, trying out the possibility of self-authored action, testing the inextricability of our dependence upon a presiding deity. Elsewhere, suicide is the natural conclusion to a romantic narrative, encapsulating the self-effacement implicated in loving another and the dissolution of erotic consummation...In suicide, the loving couple expresses their mutual self-sacrifice and interdependence, while the solitary subject appropriates its reflexive activity in tragically limited imitation of their indivisible double identity. (Langley 2009: 253)

That is to say, with Shakespeare, suicide turns into the act of an inward-looking selfhood where self-destruction is also an ontological and aesthetic desire for subjectivity. As Richard Sanderson points out: 'One of the achievements of English Renaissance tragedy is to have so "diligently surveyed" the moral, psychological, and aesthetic dimensions of "Self-Homicide"' (Sanderson 1992: 212). This is amply demonstrated in the works of Shakespeare, who situates the suicides of characters like Romeo, Juliet, Brutus, Othello, Antony and Cleopatra within the broader human context of the ethical, emotional and existential question of self-destruction. Not surprisingly, Shakespeare approaches the problem of suicide by focusing on its positive as well as negative aspects, often simultaneously. In his Roman plays, suicide is most often mentioned, in Roman spirit, as an honourable death, as in the following passage of *Antony and Cleopatra*:

> It is great
> To do that thing that ends all other deeds,
> Which shackles accidents and bolts up change.
>
> (Shakespeare 1836: 705)

We recognise a similar approach in Brutus' reflections on suicide in *Julius Caesar*. When Cassius asks Brutus what he plans to do if they lose the battle against Octavius and Antony, Brutus replies:

> Even by the rule of that philosophy
> By which I did blame Cato for the death
> Which he did give himself—I know not how,
> But I do find it cowardly and vile,
> For fear of what might fall, so to prevent
> The time of life—arming myself with patience
> To stay the providence of some high powers
> That govern us below.
>
> (Shakespeare 1836: 677)

While he brilliantly dramatises the difficulty of suicide as a moral choice for a noble man like Brutus, it is interesting to see that Shakespeare does not turn Brutus into a Stoic. On the contrary, despite Brutus' historical admiration for Cato (who as we know committed suicide in 46 BC), Shakespeare turns Brutus' suicide into a non-sanctified act. Perhaps because, confronted with the historical Brutus who committed suicide, and having declared his allegiance to monarchism, Shakespeare decided 'to portray Brutus in as favorable a light as possible, suppressed his Stoical conclusions and made him into a quasi-Christian, or at least into a quasi-Christian Platonist' (Sacharoff 1972: 122), thereby also reminding us of

'Hamlet's reasoning that "no man ought to inflict on himself a voluntary death, thinking to escape temporary ills, lest he find himself among ills that are unending"' (ibid.: 119).

Consequently, in Shakespearean tragedies, suicide is not a hasty decision: it is a matter of conscience. The essence of Macbeth's suffering is that he cannot escape his conscience. He comes to see his life, stained by murder, as 'full of sound and fury/Signifying nothing' (Shakespeare 1836: 325). Indeed, in Shakespeare's profoundly moral universe, suicide is always carefully dramatised as an act of conscience as he demonstrates the workings of moral judgment even in this most 'selfish' of human acts. Shakespearean tragedies offer no immediate or easy answers to the questions raised by the problem of suicide. 'They suggest no guarantee of success or promise of heavenly reward for those who struggle...to act in accordance with their own judgment. But the enactments of tragic self-discovery do suggest that any attempt to evade or simplify the operation of conscience is a violation of the self...' (Slights 1981: 132). Neither do they succeed in sweeping away the Augustinian blame and reprobation of suicide.

To approach and analyse the question of suicide from a non-moralistic point of view, humanity had to wait for a thinker like Michel de Montaigne and, later, eighteenth-century philosophers like David Hume and Jean-Jacques Rousseau.

> From the Renaissance to the Revolution, there were multiple modes of reflection on suicide. The decline of these diverse humanistic representations of the suicidal act and their replacement, in the nineteenth century, by academic disciplines focusing on suicide as a fact are unfortunate developments in Western thought. Not only do we understand early modern culture better when we recognize suicide as a major topic in it, we also understand suicide better when we

> look at it through the lens of early modern humanism. (Gordon 2016: 33)

This new attention given to suicide in modern times was in large part due to the new conception of the individual in modern culture, which situated suicide as one among the ordinary everyday problems of humanity. Anne Louise Germaine de Staël-Holstein, better known as Madame de Staël, was among the first women of letters in modern times to publish on suicide. In her first book entitled *On the Influence of the Passions* (1798), she supported the act of self-killing as a valid solution to human unhappiness. However, fourteen years later in 1812, she rejected her previous ideas and argued against suicide in her book *Reflections on Suicide*, giving the following explanation for her retraction: 'In my work *On the Influence of the Passions* I have applauded suicide and I have ever since repented of that inconsiderate expression. I was then in the pride and vivacity of early youth, but of what use is life, without the hope of improvement' (Madame de Staël 1816: 10, footnote). It goes without saying that Madame de Staël's observation on suicide is central to the entire debate of modern European consciousness on the issue of suicide. Moreover, she is also the heir of all the philosophical debates on suicide which took place before and after the French Revolution. Unsurprisingly, the elimination of Christian values in the French Revolution revived the question of the pursuit of happiness, and with it the problem of suicide. In *On the Influence of the Passions*, de Staël took a stand against religious fanaticism, and held that true religion presupposes an unshakeable faith. According to her, in a century of unbelief, it is only true faith that gives us the power to suffer and to die bravely. For, as she observed,

> he who can place suicide among the number of his resolves may fearlessly enter and run the career of the passions: to the passions he may consign his life,

> if he be but conscious of sufficient resolution to cut short its thread the moment that the thunderbolt of Fate shall have blasted and destroyed the object of all his wishes and of all his cares...And this, not because, under such a situation life can still have any charms, but because we must compress into one moment's space all the incentives of our grief, in order to struggle against the ever-recurring thought of death; and because misfortune spreads itself over the whole extent of life; while the terrors that suicide inspires concentrate themselves into the space of an instant: and, in order to effect the act of self-murder, a man must take in the picture of his misfortunes, like the spectacle of his final end, aided by the intense energy of one sentiment and of one single idea. (Madame de Staël 1813: 263–264)

Although she approved of the individual's courage to kill oneself in *On the Influence of the Passions*, she later renounced this idea in *Reflections on Suicide.* Invoking the message of Jesus Christ, de Staël condemned suicide, assuming that if it were permissible to kill oneself, then the precepts of the Gospels would have no foundation. She argued:

> The gift of existence is a constant miracle; the thoughts and feelings, which compose it, have something so sublime in them, that we cannot, without astonishment, contemplate our being by the aid of the faculties of this being. Shall we then squander, in a moment of impatience and ennui, the breath by which we have felt love, recognized genius, and adored the deity?...In short, if we are incapable of that Christian resignation, which makes us submit to the ordeal of life, at least we should return to the classical beauty of character of the ancients, and make glory our divinity, when we do not feel ourselves able to sacrifice this glory itself to the highest of all virtues. We believe we have shown that suicide, whose end

> is, to rid ourselves of life, carries with it no character of devotion to duty, and cannot, of course, merit the name of enthusiasm. (Madame de Staël 1816: 73)

It was probably the French Revolution and its socio-political and moral consequences that changed de Staël's thinking on suicide. As she underlined in her book,

> There are examples of suicide in the French nation, but we cannot generally attribute them to the melancholy of their character, nor to the elevation of their ideas. Positive evils have led some Frenchmen to this act, and they have committed it with intrepidity, but also with the thoughtlessness which often characterize them. Nevertheless, the multitudes of emigrants, which the revolution produced, have supported the most cruel privations with a sort of equanimity, of which no other nation would have been capable. Their genius disposes them more to action than to reflection, and this manner of life diverts them from the troubles of existence. (Madame de Staël 1816: 74–75)

It is interesting to see how a writer of the early nineteenth century like de Staël draws upon social theory to explain the phenomenon of suicide eighty years before Émile Durkheim. She followed eighteenth-century philosophy in order to relate suicide to social institutions and historical conjectures. More importantly, she stretched the moral imagination of her readers, arguably more than Durkheim would later, and reopened the religious-secular debate between Augustinian and Humean theories of suicide, which was closed by 'apostles of suicide' like Voltaire. Also, de Staël never stopped believing in the immortality of the soul.

While French Renaissance philosophers like Montaigne had already initiated an individualistic approach to the discussion of suicide, with Voltaire and his *Questions sur l'*

Encyclopédie, the debate on the morality of self-killing turned into a more philosophical and sociological one. For Voltaire, suicide was neither a moral deficiency, nor a case of having been tempted by the devil. For Voltaire, the problem of suicide is essentially a philosophical debate, which points to very concrete problems of modern society, such as the large number of suicides in the new proletarian class created by the progress of mercantile economy. But we must also add to this the phenomenon of the desacralisation of human nature by modern science and the new disenchanted approach to the problem of death. Suicide was, therefore, considered a symptom of insanity and depression, and not an act against God. Philosophers and scientists were beginning to look at suicide not as immoral or anti-religious behaviour, but a consequence of the mental state of the individual. Eighteenth-century philosophers and thinkers like Voltaire, Diderot and Rousseau were conscious of the complexities and multifaceted pressures of life in modern society, and the difficulties faced by the modern subject in struggling to find a place and an anchor within it. Voltaire, for instance, knew well that killing oneself takes great courage. Furthermore,

> The prevalence of political suicide in Rome and its disappearance in France, he suggests, may have more to do with 'fashion' than a decline in courage... [Yet] Voltaire derives no categorical conclusions, and certainly no science of suicide, from his inquiry. Nevertheless, he stretches the sociological imagination of his readers...[and] succeeds in making the[m]...appreciate the variability of suicide over time and across space, and he implies that there is no contradiction-free way to criminalize suicide. Treating suicide as neither heroic nor pathological, Voltaire opens up a considerable middle ground for potential inquiry, on both a moral and a sociological plane. (Gordon 2016: 46)

As far as modernity was concerned, suicide was neither a Stoic moral preoccupation, nor a deviation from the teachings of religion. 'Suicide moved from the governance of the (Christian) ethical-religious regime of power during the Middle Ages to becoming the focus of a medical-scientific community and of an entire apparatus of experts in the production of new knowledge' (Gupta 2005: 89). As suicide and individualism became more and more interrelated in modern society, philosophers and artists started depicting the ontological intensity of this most profound and private experience. Suicide was no longer condemned, but instead became a response, even a solution, to the emptiness and absurdity of life.

When Nietzsche wrote in *Beyond Good and Evil* that 'The thought of suicide is a powerful comfort: it helps one through many a dreadful night' (Nietzsche 2000: 281), he clearly understood that the modern subject is the master of his/her life and death. To kill oneself is to avoid a reversal of fortune. It meant accepting and respecting the philosophical and artistic function of suicide as a possibility. By committing suicide, the philosopher-artist distances him/herself from the collective representation of society. Accepting suicide as a mode of living and dying was a way of rejecting centuries of the demonisation of self-killing by conservative moralists and followers of religious doctrines. For the first time in many centuries, suicide was no longer considered a great crime against humanity and a taboo. Modernity promoted individualism, individual identity, expression and creativity, and with it came the desire and the will to author one's death. Dying by suicide became an experience deeply influenced by the modern mode of being and the primacy of the individual against the community. The will to suicide was no longer deemed a sin, but another way for the modern individual to affirm his/her freedom and selfhood in the world. What was mislaid for centuries by executioners of human education came to the forefront of the life of the modern individual. For the last hundred years, human beings have been admired not only for the ways in which they lived, but also for the ways in which they died. Here, the suicide of a writer-artist like Yukio Mishima is a resounding example, for it expresses the human will to live eternally through an aesthetisation of death. Mishima, by his life and by his art, showed us the path to the aesthetic sources of his suicide, and, through it, the access to an ultimate, if terrifying, beauty.

> His choice of an anachronistic public form of death allowed him to present himself as an ultimate Nietzschean man of action and to exit the stage as the spectacular performer that he had always been, but it also meant that his literary oeuvre would forever be read in the shadow of that final act. (Sherif 2003: 220)

For Mishima the, beauty of *seppuku* or ritual suicide in a heroic cause suggested a rebellious move away from the atomising passivity of post-war Japan. 'Only in that final moment would he know, for himself, if his action was beautiful and heroic enough, i.e. tragic enough, to nullify the distinction between art and act' (Abelsen 1996: 679). Mishima's aesthetic act of self-killing takes us back to Camus' assertion: 'There is but one truly serious philosophical problem and that is suicide'. To understand it, one needs to study the approaches to suicide through history, starting with Socrates and Seneca and ending with Mishima. In other words, the envisioning of suicide as a philosophy, as a way of (non-)being, and not just as a meaningless act or an act of extreme despair, will enable us to approach with sophistication the many complexities of the subject.

II PHILOSOPHICAL SUICIDES

Suicide was a common phenomenon among ancient civilisations. Many of these, including the Greek and the Roman, recognised suicide as the search for honour or the fear of shame. 'The Greeks generally recognized a sharp distinction between honorable and cowardly suicides' (Garrison 1991: 33). For the ancient Greeks, life *per se* was a good thing. They saw no contradiction between merely living and a good life (*eudaimonia*). Yet, as the Athenian tragedies repeatedly show us, the Greeks were equally, acutely and existentially aware of life as suffering. Despite this acceptance of the essence of life as suffering, not all schools of thought in ancient Greece accepted suicide as a legitimate act. Surprisingly, in Plato's philosophy, the preference of the soul over the body does not have, as an immediate outcome, the acceptance of suicide. Quite the opposite, in Plato's *Phaedo*, Socrates advises the sophist Euenus to die as a philosopher, but not to take his own life. There is an apparent contradiction here, which is pointed at by Cebes, who asks: 'How do you mean, Socrates, that it is not right to do oneself violence, and yet that the philosopher will be willing to follow one who is dying?' (Miles 2001: 257). However, far from assuaging the intellectual discomfort of Cebes, Socrates only adds to the complexity of the matter by underscoring his equal commitment to both principles.

According to Murray Miles, 'it appears that Plato is wrestling here, as most everywhere in the *Phaedo*, with the tensions between his Socratic inheritance and his own Pythagorean/ Orphic religious entanglements, struggling to reconcile them through a philosophical synthesis that still eludes him' (ibid.). We know for a fact that the Pythagoreans condemned suicide absolutely. We also know that Plato's Socrates was trying to point out that the Pythagorean stance was wrong. This suggests that suicide in ancient Greece was a relatively common and much-debated phenomenon, and that there existed different attitudes and perspectives on suicide in Greek society.

The central idea proposed by Socrates in Plato's *Phaedo* is that suicide is permissible if it is done on the basis of divine order; otherwise, killing oneself is prohibited by the gods. Therefore,

> If Socrates does consider himself to be about to commit suicide, we must presume that he thinks that he has had some such message or allowance—whether that came in the form of the Athenians' judgement or the dream he recounts at the beginning of the *Crito* (44a5–b5). The *Phaedo* itself offers a possible example of such a sign. Socrates' dream at 60e, by telling him to practise the arts, will also be recommending that he die, if it is understood that the specific art in question is philosophy, and philosophy is a preparation for death. (Warren 2001: 100)

History remembers the death of Socrates as a noble and exemplary act of altruism in the name of philosophy—the 'love of wisdom'. But here, one must make an important distinction: Socrates was certainly prepared to die, but not to commit suicide. His death was determined by his sentence, which was not chosen by him. Socrates, in complete consciousness of his actions, refused to evade either his trial, or his death as decreed by the trial. Socrates was, in a manner of speaking, forced to drink the hemlock, which he accepted because he was ready to die as a philosopher, for the sake of philosophy. In both Plato and Xenophon, we find Socrates portrayed as a philosopher who had no fear of death, who possessed the courage of his convictions, and who strongly believed that a Delphic oracle encouraged him to take the path of a divine mission. In his speech at the trial, Socrates explains the meaning of his mission:

> Men of Athens...as long as I draw breath...I shall not cease to practice philosophy, [and] to exhort you... in my usual way...: Good Sir, you are an Athenian, a citizen of the greatest city with the greatest reputation for both wisdom and power; are you not ashamed of your eagerness to possess as much wealth, reputation and honours as possible, while you do not care for... wisdom or truth, or the best possible state of your soul?...Be sure that this is what the god orders me to do, and I think there is no greater blessing for the city than my service to the god. (Plato 1997: 27–28)

From this passage of Plato's *Apology*, one can see that Socrates established a close relationship between his life as a philosopher and his mission of turning Athenians to the care of their souls. Socrates had a strong moral conviction that operated in the background of his philosophical vocation. His actions were thus shaped by his conviction, and by his awareness of the meaning of life and death. For Socrates, fearing death amounted to cowardice. And the fear of death, for him, resulted from ignorance. Once again, evidence of Socrates' moral courage in the face of certain death can be found in another passage of Plato's *Apology*:

> To fear death, gentlemen, is no other than to think oneself wise when one is not, to think one knows what one does not know. No one knows whether death may not be the greatest of all blessings for a man, yet men

> fear it as if they knew that it is the greatest of evils. And surely it is the most blameworthy ignorance to believe that one knows what one does not know. It is perhaps...in this respect...I shall never fear or avoid things of which I do not know... (Plato 1997: 27)

This awareness of one's ignorance is the touchstone of Socrates' philosophy of life, and his art of living and dying.

Consequently, Socrates' philosophical approach to death was completed by his view of living truthfully and nobly. He envisaged a good life as a quest for truth, virtue, morality and knowledge. Undoubtedly, he was the first Western philosopher for whom the nobility of spirit was a mode of life, a way of being. 'There were many before Socrates who lived highly moral lives, but no one before Socrates had essayed to live ethically by the application of rigorous moral reasoning' (Graham 2016: 153). Therefore, we can say that dying was also a responsible moral act, which he undertook as a philosopher and as a citizen of Athens. As an exemplar of both reason and moral virtue, Socrates represented the politically excluded voice of philosophy. Therefore, sentencing Socrates to death was also the killing of philosophy in the Greek public space. We know from Plato's dialogues that in accepting death, Socrates was acting as per the dictates of his *daimon*, his divine inner voice. What has, however, remained a mystery perhaps is that Socrates—the fountainhead of philosophical questioning, logic and reasoning—never once questioned the verdict of his death, or the act of drinking the hemlock. When we look at Jacques-Louis David's landmark painting, *The Death of Socrates*, we realise that there is something more to Socrates' death—at the heart of it is an act of profound philosophical dissent, expressed as a message to future philosophers who aspire to live truthful, meaningful, worthwhile lives, and who aspire to live by their beliefs. Socrates, who by his life and by his death, became a role model for the whole of humanity, particularly for twentieth-century nonviolent practitioners like Gandhi and Martin Luther King, Jr., is none other than an individual in quest of self-perfection and 'an examined life'. In choosing to drink the hemlock, Socrates showed once again his determination to express his indifference to death and absence of fear until the very end—as a philosophical lesson for the future history of thought. 'His death at the age of seventy was intended by him as an act of philosophical martyrdom that would allow future philosophy to be favorably regarded as a source of courage and justice' (Smith 2012: 34).

Greek thinkers contemporary to Socrates, and those who came after him, were well aware of his stature as the quintessential philosopher. 'According to Philodemus, the Stoics actually wanted to be called "Socratics"' (Long 1988: 151). The Stoics turned constantly to the writings of Plato and Xenophon to find in Socrates, as Cicero says, 'the first [who] called down philosophy from heaven to earth' (Cicero 1927: V, iv, 1–3). Yet, their views on suicide differed occasionally from that of Socrates. Unlike Socrates, who did not advocate what the cynic Diogenes called 'reason or the rope' (*logon e brochon*), the Stoics recommended suicide as an alternative to a life without virtue. However, while the early Stoics were not obsessed with the idea of suicide, they recommended it in certain circumstances. 'Some Stoics turned occasionally to the idea of a divine calling which Socrates had already used as a justification in the *Phaedo* (62C): it is wrong to leave life, to forsake our post in the world, unless God calls us' (Seidler 1983: 432).

Roman philosophers, on the other hand, were haunted by the idea of suicide. Among the Roman Stoics, Seneca has written extensively on suicide, especially in his *Epistulae ad Lucilium*. According to Pierluigi Donini, 'the glorification of suicide as the supreme and perhaps only act of freedom on man's part is a peculiarity of Seneca, which has no parallel in the previous tradition' (Donini 1999: 735). Interestingly, Seneca himself had a 'Socratic' death, being forced by Emperor Nero to take his own life. But years before his death, the young Seneca was already attracted to the subject of annihilating the self, and once in his youth, he had even decided to commit suicide.

Seneca's philosophy of suicide was not separate from his Stoic philosophy of life and death, which he shared with another Stoic thinker, Epictetus. They both believed that suicide could be a road to freedom. But in the case of Seneca, killing oneself was also an antidote to the miseries of life; dying well was a remedy to living badly. Furthermore, for Seneca, suicide could be a journey towards possible glory, and 'the highway to liberty', to which the individual could aspire. As he challenges his readers in this passage from *De Ira* (3.15.4):

> In whatever direction you may turn your eyes, there lies the means to end our woes. See you that precipice? Down that is the way to liberty. See you that sea, that river, that well? There sits liberty—at the bottom. See you that tree, stunted, blighted, and barren? Yet from its branches hangs liberty. See you that throat of yours, your gullet, your heart? They are ways of escape from servitude. Are the ways of egress I show you too toilsome, do they require too much courage and strength? Do you ask what is the highway to liberty? Any vein in your body! (Seneca 1928: 38)

Seneca found nothing more ignoble than not having the choice to kill oneself. Unlike Socrates, he did not think that an individual should ask the gods for death. For Seneca, living the full life of a Stoic also meant having full control over one's life—including the choice and the freedom of ending it. He therefore believed that

> A man who sluggishly awaits his fate is almost a coward, just as he is immoderately given to wine who

> drains the jar dry and sucks up even the dregs. But we shall ask this question also: 'Is the extremity of life the dregs, or is it the clearest and purest part of all, provided only that the mind is unimpaired, and the senses, still sound, give their support to the spirit, and the body is not worn out and dead before its time?' For it makes a great deal of difference whether a man is lengthening his life or his death. (Seneca 2016a: 128)

Like Socrates, in order to practise the art of living, Seneca also considered it immensely important to free oneself from the fear of death, especially because life is short, and 'You are living as if destined to live for ever' (Seneca 1997). In his essay *On the Shortness of Life*, he brilliantly captures what has always been a central human predicament and preoccupation, and is perhaps truer now than ever before:

> you don't notice how much time has already passed, but squander it as though you had a full and overflowing supply...You act like mortals in all that you fear, and like immortals in all that you desire. You will hear many people saying: 'When I am fifty I shall retire into leisure...' And what guarantee do you have of a longer life?...Aren't you ashamed to keep for yourself just the remnants of your life...? How late it is to begin really to live just when life must end! How stupid to forget our mortality, and put off sensible plans to our fiftieth and sixtieth years...! (Seneca 1997: 5)

Seneca was convinced that a philosopher was entitled to decide about his life and death. He counseled neither an escape from life, nor an indifference to death. On the contrary, he advocated an examined and worthwhile life in the Socratic mode. For him, an individual had a right not to suffer, by ending his/her life. 'This is the one reason why we cannot complain of life: it keeps no one against his will. Humanity is well situated, because no man is unhappy except by his own fault. Live, if you so desire; if not, you may return to the place whence you came' (Seneca 2017: 40). It is important to see how Seneca associated the encounter with death with a sense of responsibility. The core question is, therefore, that in Seneca's philosophy, responsibility offers a perspective on individual agency with regard to life and death. Seneca's ethic of responsibility, here expressed as the notion of 'fault', provides a framework for approaching the act of suicide. This thoughtfulness about life and death takes in Seneca the form of an attentive responsiveness to the boredom and suffering of the world—a philosophical vision that we will find eighteen centuries later in a philosopher like Arthur Schopenhauer. For both philosophers, living per se is nothing but suffering. In his famous *Letter 70 to Lucilius*, Seneca sketches what he understands by living:

> Merely to live is not in itself good, but rather, to live well. Thus the sage will live as long as he thought, not as long as he can. He'll examine where he will live, with whom, and how, and what he will do. He'll think about what kind of life is his, not what length. If a host of troubles arise and roil his serenity, he'll set himself free; and he won't do this only in the final exigency...He judges that it makes no difference whether he fashions his end or receives it...whether one dies sooner, or later; dying well or badly is what matters. (Seneca 2018: 76–77)

Letter 70 to Lucilius reveals another facet of Seneca's moral philosophy, which is more Greek than Roman in nature. As we understand Seneca, for him, the aim of life was moral perfectibility. In other words, the love of wisdom aims at the improvement of one's life. Seneca, therefore, considered life a philosophical project. Undoubtedly, from Seneca's point of view, suicide was part of this philosophical journey. That is to say, he did not consider suicide the act of a desperate mind, but a philosophical gesture towards individual freedom. Seneca defined freedom as the power of self-determination.

> I have set freedom before my eyes; and I am striving for that reward. And what is freedom, you ask? It means not being a slave to any circumstance, to any constraint, to any chance; it means compelling Fortune to enter the lists on equal terms. And on the day when I know that I have the upper hand, her power will be naught. When I have death in my own control, shall I take orders from her? (Seneca 2016b: 114)

But, in the manner of other Stoics, Seneca also believed that only the wise man was truly free. It was the moral courage and the capacity to distinguish between good and evil which enabled the wise individual not to do anything against his/her will. As Seneca proclaimed:

> What evil is there in torture, or in other things we call adversities? This, I think: that the mind gives way, bends, and collapses. None of these things can happen to the wise man. He stands upright under any load. Nothing diminishes him. None of these things that he must endure bothers him. He does not complain when anything that can befall man has befallen him. He knows his own strength. (Seneca 2016c: 186)

Seneca believed that the best way to gain freedom was to have moral courage against evil, but also to be always sure that we have the option to die when we want. However, he saw a difference between the suicide of a wise man and an ordinary man taking the path of a virtuous life.

> The wise man is completely free: he can hold out as long as he wants under torture, and never gives way. He will always see virtue as the only good, vice

> as the only evil, no matter how painful the torture. His suicide is always a free choice. Those making progress towards virtue do not act with the same freedom. They view the pain as the wise man does, but their opinion about it is not unshakeable. They cannot argue against the body forever. But they can, thanks to suicide, preserve their virtue by departing life before their minds give way. (Englert 1990: 19)

It should be pointed out that Seneca did not consider the act of suicide to be an act of despair. On the contrary, he was of the opinion that the wise relied solely upon their moral courage and freedom, to live as well as to die. Thus, in Seneca's philosophy, the autonomous character of the wise always prevailed. The other important principle for him was to accept life as long as it was worth living, but also not fear to replace life by death when it ceased to be so. According to Seneca, neither fear nor suffering, nor disgust with life are sufficient motives for committing suicide. And even for the wise, suicide is more than just killing oneself—it is an act of self-examination. For Seneca, this self-examination was an expression of the moral courage to die, but also proof that the wise man had a 'duty' to live well.

> Stoics called for doing one's duty, so faced even with death...This came to mean a willingness to die even if it was not necessary...One should leave life as one leaves a room that has become too smoky. The Stoics considered this to be strength, but from our perspective, such a suicide might seem rather to indicate weakness, a choice not to bear the difficulty of life. With the Stoics, the weight was never on actually committing suicide but rather on not fearing death. Nevertheless, Stoicism has been famously connected to the tolerance of suicide. (Hecht 2013: 31)

Unlike Seneca, the Epicurean philosophers, who lived during the Hellenistic period and early Roman era, considered suicide a form of weakness. But, like the Stoics, they were of the opinion that death should be contemplated and accepted with calm and serenity. Epicurus thought that death does not look us in the face, because when we exist, it does not exist, and when it exists, we no longer exist. Here is a passage from a letter of Epicurus in which he expressed his opinion about death:

> Whatsoever causes no annoyance when it is present causes only a groundless pain in the expectation. Death, therefore, the most awful of evils, is nothing to us, seeing that, when we are, death is not come, and when death is come, we are not. It is nothing then, either to the living or to the dead, for with the living it is not and the dead exist no longer. (Reale 1985: 173)

Epicurus advised his friends and followers not to fear death, but he did not consider suicide as a reasonable way to die. 'He suggested that people who choose suicide do so because they grow tired of the vicissitudes and tedium of life, and weary of their fear of dying' (Hecht 2013: 34). Readers of Epicurus and the Epicureans know well that for them wisdom was the possession of happiness, and they considered happiness to be found in pleasure. As such, they rejected anything that disrupted this journey to the principles of pleasure, whether it was pain in the body, trouble in the soul or suicide. Where someone like Seneca suggested suicide as a remedy to pain and suffering, the Epicureans suggested resistance to pain. The Roman Epicurean Lucretius, who authored the long poem *On the Nature of Things* (*De Natura Rerum*), and who committed suicide at the age forty-five in 55 BCE, dismissed death in the following lines:

> ...death is nothing to us and does not concern us at all...We felt no dismay in times gone by when from all directions the Carthaginians came to fight, when

> the whole world was shaken in a quivering ferment of war...no one knew whether power over all human affairs on land and sea would fall to this side or that. In just the same way...when body and spirit, which together make up our single self, are separated, absolutely nothing will be able to happen to us...since we will not be alive at that point... (De May 2009: 72–73)

The philosophical verses of Lucretius had a great impact on the modern writers and thinkers of the sixteenth and eighteenth centuries. We find one hundred forty-nine quotations from *De Natura Rerum* in Montaigne's *Essays*. Montaigne went back to the idea of death in Lucretius and underlined the idea that the death of the individual causes the mask he has worn all his life to fall off. Montaigne's idea, borrowed from Lucretius, was to fight against the fear of death, rather than fear death itself. Both Montaigne and Lucretius saw death as a part of life, and not necessarily as something external to or out of life. As Montaigne observed, life and death are part of the same passage and journey.

> Death is the origin of another life...just so did we strip off our former veil when we entered it...Long life and short life are made all one by death. For there is no long or short for things that are no more...But nature forces us to it. Go out of this world, she says, as you entered it. The same passage that you made from death to life, without feeling or fright, make it again from life to death. Your death is a part of the order of the universe; it is a part of the life of the world. (Montaigne 1965: 64)

We find hereby a Montaigne who was not only a follower of the ancient wisdom of the Greeks and Romans in general, but also an acute reader of Lucretius in particular. Yet the Christian essence of Montaigne's thought cannot be ignored when he reflected on God or on death. As he pointed out: 'It is for our Christian faith, and not for Stoic virtue, to aspire to that divine and miraculous metamorphosis' (Montaigne 1965: 457). One needs to accept Montaigne as he was—fearful of death and full of metaphysical anxiety. But what separated him from the ancient philosophers like Socrates, Seneca and Lucretius was Christianity, and its moral view on suicide. Christianity replaced the concept of 'shame' by that of 'sin'. 'The prominent Greek and Roman suicides were typically people who were being told—often by legal authority—to kill themselves' (Hecht 2013: 24). These were predominantly philosophical suicides, a rare phenomenon among modern philosophers.

Even those modern philosophers who approved of suicide as a legitimate act did not commit suicide. As for those who opposed suicide in modern times, they were for the most part influenced by Christian doctrine. It was the controversy with Stoicism that led Christian thinkers like Saint Augustine to condemn suicide. Among the early Christians, there were sects, like the Donatists in North Africa, who approved of the act of suicide. Augustine's rejection of suicide was a theoretical and philosophical response to both the Donatists and the Stoics. For Augustine suicide was a crime, everywhere and always. He believed that killing oneself was like killing another human being. He wrote:

> And as for those who would not put an end to their lives, lest they might seem to escape the crime of another by a sin of their own, he who lays this to their charge as a great wickedness is himself not guiltless... For if it is not lawful to...slay even a guilty person, whose death no public sentence has warranted, then certainly he who kills himself is a homicide, and so much the guiltier of his own death, as he was more innocent of that offence for which he doomed himself to die. (St. Augustine of Hippo 2015: 20)

Saint Augustine was not only addressing the Romans against the blame that Christianity is weak, but also writing for future Christians, confirming the fact that suicide is contrary to the natural inclination of man, and contrary to natural law. This is why he writes in his magnum opus, *De Citate Dei*, 'But this we affirm, this we maintain, this we every way pronounce to be right, that no man ought to inflict on himself voluntary death, for this is to escape the ills of time by plunging into those of eternity' (St. Augustine of Hippo 2012–2017: 33). Expanding on Augustine's ideas, during the Middle Ages the Christian church strongly and completely rejected suicide as being against nature. 'In life as well as literature, Christian religious practice in the high Middle Ages was to condemn suicides...The ferocity of the response to suicide can seem unbelievable, but examples from across Europe span several centuries' (Hecht 2013: 56). Humanity had to wait several centuries before the idea of suicide could be contemplated, philosophically and otherwise, once again.

III SUICIDE AND MODERNITY

Through human history, it may be argued that philosophy has, in general, been far more tolerant and accommodating of suicide than religion. Religious thinkers across cultures and time have never approved of suicide as a way of ending life, given to humankind by God. Christian thinkers like Augustine and Dante rejected all forms of tolerance of the philosophical suicides of antiquity. While the ancient Greeks and Romans not only contemplated but debated different aspects of the philosophical problem of suicide, it was condemned and punished as a sin in medieval Europe. With the rise of modern science, and its new human-centric understanding of life and death, believers and non-believers, philosophers and scientists alike started looking at suicide afresh from different perspectives. The changing political, economic, and intellectual climate in modern Europe also prepared the new social, cultural and aesthetic context for a change of understanding regarding suicide.

> The more that philosophers and philosophical clubs became synonymous with antireligious attitudes and renewed interest in the ancients, the more these people and places were connected to tolerance or encouragement of suicide. Just as religious writing had used the ancient suicides as a counterpoint, the

> new secular writing used ancient heroes to valorize self-murder. (Hecht 2013: 94)

Modernity secularised both life and death, and with it the act of suicide. Taking one's life for social or personal reasons was no more considered a sin. Many modern writers, artists and philosophers took a stance on the issue of suicide, and argued for it more passionately than those in pagan antiquity.

Émile Durkheim's sociological monograph, *Le Suicide*, published in 1897, is considered even today a classic in European sociology. To understand its continuing relevance, it is necessary to place this work in the context of its time. Durkheim's sociological inquiry showed, for instance, that in late nineteenth-century Europe, more people committed suicide in the city than in the countryside, that more men committed suicide than women, that more single individuals took their lives than those married, and that more people killed themselves in times of peace than in times of war. Durkheim's studies also led him to the conclusion that more Protestants committed suicide as compared to Catholics and Jews. Clearly, as a sociologist, Durkheim was not interested in the philosophical essence or problem of suicide. What concerned him were rather the social and communal human bonds that existed in modern industrial societies. To that end, he therefore established a typology of the different forms of suicide, distinguishing between four kinds: egoistic, altruistic, anomic and fatalistic.

> Egoistic suicide occurs in a person who lacks a sense of belonging to the community and who becomes overcome by feelings of meaninglessness, apathy, and depression. Altruistic suicide is the opposite: the victim is so profoundly enmeshed in the ideals of the group that upholding these ideals becomes more important than life itself. Anomic suicide is characterized by an individual's moral confusion,

> uncertainty, and lack of direction, usually related to dramatic social and economic upheaval. Fatalist suicide is the opposite of anomic: it is a response to being chronically oppressed so that one's own desires are endlessly thwarted. (Hecht 2013: 194)

For Durkheim, while anomic suicide underscored certain disturbances in modern societies that lead individuals to hope too much, egoistic suicide was the direct result of a lack of social integration. This is why, according to Durkheim, more Protestants committed suicide as compared to Catholics, because their approach to faith gives more weight to the individual than to the community. He further concluded that 'Suicide varies inversely with the degree of integration of the social groups of which the individual forms a part' (Durkheim 1951: 209).

Durkheim was also well aware of the relationship between French literary romanticism and romantic ideas about suicide, especially in the works of Lamartine and Chateaubriand. He referred to Lamartine's *Raphael* as an expression of egoistic suicide and to Chateaubriand's *René* as an example of anomic suicide. In Durkheim's understanding,

> While Raphael is a creature of meditation who finds his ruin within himself, René is the insatiate type. 'I am accused,' he exclaims unhappily, 'of being inconstant in my desires, of never long enjoying the same fancy, of being prey to an imagination eager to sound the depth of my pleasures as though it were overwhelmed by their persistence; I am accused of always missing the goal I might attain. Alas! I only seek an unknown good, the instinct for which pursues me. Is it my fault if I everywhere find limits, if everything once experienced has no value for me? (Durkheim 1951: 286–287)

That is to say, Durkheim did not necessarily relate suicide to insanity or mental imbalance. On the contrary, from his point of view, suicide, as analysed sociologically, was a modern phenomenon and closely related to the rise of industrial societies. According to Hecht,

> Durkheim attached incalculable importance to the disappearance of the small town and of the closer relations people had before city industry, trains, and changing mores separated the average person from his community. People feel integrated through family, community, and the state, and modernity supplied less community than earlier periods...People cannot become attached to higher aims if they do not feel they belong to anything. Thus, for Durkheim, freeing people from all social pressure abandons them to themselves, and to sorrow. So it seems that for people sensitive to melancholia some kind of deeper sense of belonging is necessary, though difficult. (Hecht 2013: 196)

Therefore, Durkheim considered that the increase in suicide throughout the nineteenth century was an indication of the weakening of the old frameworks of sociability. For Durkheim, suicide was the effect of social factors alone. He therefore did not apply the rules of his method to the analysis of physiological or psychological factors. We can see how Durkheim links the individual and the society of which the individual is part, though he frames the individual as the point of reference, because when situations and social contexts change, especially for the worse, according to him, individual decisions may also change. Durkheim, therefore, concludes that:

> A man who kills himself...does wrong only to himself and there is no occasion for the intervention of

> society; for so goes the ancient maxim Volenti non fit injuria. This is an error. Society is injured because the sentiment is offended on which its most respected moral maxims today rest...How could this sentiment maintain the least authority if the moral conscience did not protest its violation?...No matter that the guilty person and the victim are one and the same; the social evil springing from the act is not affected merely by the author being the one who suffers. (Durkheim 1951: 337)

As a modern, Durkheim did not consider suicide to be an act of nature, but, on the contrary, as a sign of social morbidity. For him, suicide was not an expression of individual liberty, but an abuse of individualism. In view of this, Durkheim's study on suicide stands out as a classic on the subject. In fact,

> *Le Suicide* remains the best sociological work on suicide, primarily because of the ideal of scientific investigation of social phenomena which it is built on and because in the final analysis it broke with the positivistic tradition of research on suicide, the tradition which was so antithetical to the treatment of suicide as actions caused by social meaning. (Douglas 1967: 76)

A careful reading of Durkheim's *Le Suicide* reveals an influence of Schopenhauer's philosophy. Durkheim largely relied on Schopenhauer's pessimistic representation of life to describe the central features of modern society, especially with reference to the subject of suicide.

> In reviewing Schopenhauer's very brief discussion of suicide, one of the things that becomes apparent is that it is replete with historical and anthropological examples of suicide in ancient and pre-modern societies, and that Schopenhauer's examples constitute explicit cases of socially induced forms

> of suicide when compared to the anthropological studies used by Durkheim in his 1897 work. (Morrison 1998: 118)

Schopenhauer called death 'the true inspiring genius, or the muse of philosophy' (Schopenhauer 1964: 249). According to him, the certainty of death and the fear that human beings have of it lead them to a metaphysical contemplation of their mortality. And therefore, 'All religious and philosophical systems are principally directed to this end, and are thus primarily the antidote to the certainty of death, which the reflective reason produces out of its own means' (ibid.). He invites the individual to reflect upon the totality of which a human being is a part, and that is the 'will to live'. For Schopenhauer, death is a part of life, although most of us most of the time continue living without stopping to think about the truth of death. 'Schopenhauer "recommends" death, in that it brings to an end individual life, which is nothing but an error (as all individuality is a unique error) and whose content is earthly thoughts and endless worries...' (Dagan 2001: 78). Schopenhauer's approach to death, including his thoughts on suicide, is a reminder of the Stoic approach to taking one's life. The Stoic philosophers considered suicide a rational act if it was made in response to difficult situations like poverty, illness or extreme pain and suffering. In a somewhat similar fashion, Schopenhauer links the act of suicide to what he calls 'the terrors of life':

> It will generally be found that where the terrors of life come to outweigh the terrors of death a man will put an end to his life. But the terrors of death offer considerable resistance...the body...is a deterrent... The struggle with that...is..., however, not as hard as it may seem...the reason is the antagonism between spiritual and physical suffering. For when we are in great or chronic physical pain we are indifferent to

> all other troubles...In the same way, great spiritual suffering makes us insensible to physical pain...It is this which makes suicide easier... (Schopenhauer 1970: 78–79)

In Schopenhauer's philosophy, suicide is a human choice, so it has nothing to do with God or religion. Also, for Schopenhauer, the fact that individuals are governed by and subordinate to the 'will to live' (or not to live) meant that suicide was not related to or impacted by the social order or context in which individuals existed. Therefore, Schopenhauer also disregards all religious morality that considers suicide a sin.

Of course, not all modern philosophers analysed suicide in the same manner as Schopenhauer. The Anglo-Irish philosopher Bishop George Berkeley rejected suicide as an immoral act since he believed that the increase of suicides in modern Europe was linked to the growth of a secular mode of thinking. In his book *Alciphron or, The Minute Philosophy: An Apology for the Christian Religion Against Those Who Are Called Freethinkers*, written in 1732, Berkeley attacked the philosophers of the Enlightenment for supporting irreligion and reducing life and death to a state of animality.

Berkeley's defense of Christian philosophy is not exactly what David Hume had in mind when he wrote his essay 'On Suicide' in 1755. Though the essay was published in 1777, after Hume's death, it was widely read and had a great impact on the spirit of the Enlightenment. In his essay, Hume criticises the idea of 'sanctity of life' as upheld by religious philosophers like Berkeley and supports the idea that suicide is a morally legitimate act. One of Hume's key arguments was to underline that 'only superstition could prevent a suicide-prone person from taking his own life, once he had freed himself of the natural fear of death...Hume effectively dismisses the possibility that we might have non-superstitious reasons for rejecting suicide, even if we do not fear death' (Merrill 1999:

397). Proclaiming his position as an agnostic philosopher, Hume asks the question: is a man who decides to take his life because he is tired of living defying divine providence? His answer is very similar to what Schopenhauer, who incidentally was an acute reader of Hume, provides some years later. According to Hume,

> The lives of men depend upon the same laws as the lives of all other animals, and these are subjected to the general laws of matter and motion...is a man's disposing of his life criminal, because in every case it is criminal to encroach upon these laws...? But this seems absurd. All animals...have full authority as far as their power extends, to alter all the operations of nature. Without the exercise of this authority they could not subsist a moment...therefore...we find that...it is no encroachment on the office of providence to disturb or alter these general laws. (Hume 2006: 378–379)

Overall, Hume is of the opinion that suicide is morally acceptable, since the one who commits suicide is not doing any harm to anyone else. But at the same time, it is undeniable that he or she is also not doing society any good. Hume's response here is that one does not, typically, commit suicide if one has a life worth living, and that therefore, 'suicide may often be consistent with interest and with our duty to ourselves', especially in instances where 'age, sickness, or misfortune, may render life a burden, and make it worse even than annihilation. I believe that no man ever threw away life while it was worth keeping' (Hume 2006: 382).

Though Hume is not famous for his essay *On Suicide*, it is undeniable that his ideas on the subject are worthy of attention, and the essay should definitely be taken seriously by anyone studying the canon of ideas on suicide. Schopenhauer was not the only European philosopher who read Hume's essay on suicide, but not everyone shared his enthusiasm about it. For Schopenhauer,

> The most thorough refutation [of the reasons against suicide] has been furnished by Hume in his essay *On Suicide*, which first appeared after his death and was at once suppressed in England by the disgraceful bigotry and scandalous power of the parsons...that a purely philosophical essay, coldly and rationally refuting the current reasons against suicide and coming from one of the leading thinkers and authors of England [sic.] had to be secretly smuggled through that country like a forbidden thing until it found a refuge abroad, brings great discredit to the English nation. (Schopenhauer 1974: 309)

Schopenhauer, as mentioned previously, appreciates Hume's non-moralistic view of suicide. But, like Hume, he also believes that there are laws of nature that govern our existence and our behaviour. In other words, taking one's life in order to escape from a painful existence is morally acceptable for him. However, this was not Immanuel Kant's position. For him, suicide was against the moral law.

Kant rejected suicide, not on the basis of religious reasons, but because he believed that suicide defied and disobeyed the law of nature, which had for its goal the preservation of life. As he underlined in the *Groundwork of the Metaphysic of Morals*, 'a system of nature by whose law the very same feeling whose function is to stimulate the furtherance of life should actually destroy life would contradict itself and consequently could not subsist as a system of nature' (Kant 1964a: 89). In addition to this, Kant argues that suicide as a form of self-love failed to generate a harmony of ends. Kant developed this idea more clearly in his *Metaphysical Principles of Virtue*:

> Man cannot deprive himself of his personality so long as one speaks of duties, thus so long as one lives...To

> destroy the subject of morality in his own person is tantamount to obliterating from the world, as far as he can, the very existence of morality itself; but morality is, nevertheless, an end in itself. Accordingly, to dispose of oneself as a mere means to some end of one's own liking is to degrade the humanity in one's person, which after all, was entrusted to man to preserve. (Kant 1964b: 83–84)

So, Kant's argument was to refute suicide as an act which went against the law of nature and against morality. In other words, for him, suicide put into question the very idea of being human and the dignity of human nature, which he considered as much higher values than the self-interest of a particular person. For Kant, therefore, the freedom to end one's life was a false freedom. He never approached the problem of suicide from the angle of the painful existence of a suffering individual. Kant's arguments for the wrongness of suicide are, however, unacceptable, because outlawing assisted suicide or suicide is to limit a human being's fundamental existential freedom.

If there is one philosopher in the nineteenth century for whom death plays a vital role in philosophy and in life, it is Søren Kierkegaard. For Kierkegaard, death is the only finality and certainty in the lives of human beings. As he writes in *Three Discourses on Imagined Occasions*: 'Death is indefinable—the only certainty, and the only thing about which nothing is certain' (Kierkegaard 1993: 91). From this perspective, Kierkegaard argues that death 'makes everyone equal, equally poor, equally powerless, equally miserable' (ibid. 1990: 185). From another perspective, in *Either/Or*, Kierkegaard analyses the situation of a young aesthete in despair as that of a hopeless individual who is unable to die, because he has not fully lived. As such, for Kierkegaard, unlike for Kant, death is a universe constantly present in life and which influences life and the living permanently. As he proclaims in *Either/Or*: 'No one returns from the dead, no one has come into the world without weeping; no one asks one if one wants to come in, none when one wants to go out' (Kierkegaard 1987: 26). Certainly, as a transcendentalist, Kierkegaard believed that the individual should deny him/herself and 'die to the world'; otherwise there is no meaning to life. In the eyes of Kierkegaard, therefore, death is the truth of existence. That is also one reason why he considered 'suffering' as the highest form of relationship with God, and escaping that suffering as what he called 'miserable wisdom'. Because where there is no suffering, there is also no consciousness of eternity. So, for Kierkegaard, emulating the Christ is to suffer like Christ, not to commit suicide. Kierkegaard would certainly

> reject the idea that his faith is a suicide of lucidity, since the leap [of faith] is precisely grounded in a fidelity to the perception of the meaninglessness of our condition. And yet there is a sense in which he also calls the leap a suicide, or a 'dying to the world', a revocation of our trust in reason to save us and a dying away to the lure of seeking comfort in the quotidian reality of 'the finite.' (Berthold 2013: 139)

Here then we have our *either/or*: either faith or suicide. To have faith, for Kierkegaard, is to 'die to the world' *without* committing suicide. To take the leap of faith is, in fact, to resist despair, suicide and meaninglessness. In Kierkegaard's universe, faith is undeniably 'an act of revolt: faith is a defiance of the darkness and despair and sense of impotence of the stranger in a strange world, and an insistence on our capacity to live here and now...' (Berthold 2013: 148). But what if God does not enter the equation? Should human beings therefore capitulate into meaninglessness and commit suicide? This is the question which becomes the touchstone for Camus' philosophy.

Camus opens *The Myth of Sisyphus* with the following words:

> There is but one truly serious philosophical problem, and that is suicide. Judging whether life is or is not worth living amounts to answering the fundamental question of philosophy. All the rest—whether or not the world has three dimensions, whether the mind has nine or twelve categories—comes afterwards. (Camus 1955: 3)

For Camus, unlike Durkheim, the essential task is not to analyse suicide as a social phenomenon, but to examine the question of the meaninglessness of existence. For Camus, though we constantly live with the absurd and confront the absurd, life is not worthless. And despite all that we suffer in life, to commit suicide is an 'insult to existence'. In other words, what is important to Camus is the very experience of being alive and to acknowledge life, even if it is short and full of trials and absurdity. Camus insists that there is a reason for us to get through despair and endure suffering in life, because at the end of it we realise that living is a rich experience. 'This is why suicide is anathema to his philosophy of the absurd experience. He says that people consider suicide the ultimate revolt, but the contrary is true. Life in the face of its pain, he writes, is the ultimate revolt' (Hecht 2013: 202). Camus' ontology of suicide is based on the struggle between the human search for meaning in life and the unbearable silence of the world. Therefore, the truth of humankind is not to commit suicide, but to learn to live with the absurd. In other words, what Camus is in essence exhorting us to do is to deal with the problem of ethics in a world without God. This is what distinguishes Camus from a Kierkegaard or a Berkeley. For Camus, if a man decides not to kill himself, it is because an individual human life has value—and not because suicide is a sin. Camus rejects suicide because he comes to the conclusion that life is, in and of itself, valuable and worth living. It is because life is valuable that revolt has a meaning. For Camus, human solidarity refers to a moral Archimedian point, which is: 'I rebel, therefore, we exist' (Camus 1956: 22). The phrase reminds us that Camus rooted his idea of compassionate justice in the refusal of the murder of oneself or the other. However, if life is valuable, we also need to pay a price for our passion for life—this, according to Camus, is the price of absurdity. As Germaine Brée underlines:

> The absurd for Camus requires no other universe than our daily world, our earth as we see it, our fellow men, ourselves. Thus integrated into our daily lives, it can be faced at every moment and, by our action, denied. Our revolt against the absurd begins when our consciousness of its existence is followed by the refusal to be obsessed and paralyzed by it. (Brée 1964: 210–211)

We can find here the roots of Camus' protest against the death penalty. The argument against suicide put forward by Camus also points to his argument against the death penalty and the murder of a condemned man. Here, as Camus might say, the choice is to save an individual life and not historical necessity—another proof that, beyond suicide and murder, Camus wants to return to the dignity of Man, of being human. His disgust of the guillotine and capital punishment are the essential leitmotifs that we can discover in many of Camus' writings. In his famous essay against the death penalty, *Reflections on the Guillotine*, Camus starts by talking about his father's reaction upon witnessing the public beheading of a convicted murderer.

> He got up in the dark to go to the place of execution at the other end of town amid a great crowd...What he saw that morning he never told anyone. My mother relates merely that he came rushing home, his face

> distorted, refused to talk, lay down for a moment on the bed, and suddenly began to vomit. He had just discovered the reality hidden under the noble phrases with which it was masked. Instead of...the slaughtered children, he could think of nothing but that quivering body that had just been dropped onto a board to have its head cut off. (Camus 1960: 175)

Despite Camus' stance against the violence of death and the death penalty, he is often most remembered for the importance he gave the question of suicide. But in fact his passion for life and for being alive is only consistent with his abhorrence of capital punishment and suicide. Also, Camus has always criticised the hypocritical role of the State and the public on the issue of violent death. Therefore, from Camus' point of view, resistance to suicide or state murder becomes a moral resistance against fatalism, because as he affirms,

> We don't think badly because we are murderers. We are murderers because we think badly. That's how you can be a murderer apparently without ever having killed. And so, more or less, we are all murderers. The first thing to do is therefore to reject, pure and simple by thought and action, any form of realistic and fatalistic thought. It is the work of each of us. (Camus 2017: 50; translation by the author)

We can add to this that from the Camusian perspective, to commit suicide is to think badly about life. Hence, in the eyes of Camus, there is no equivalence between a revengeful retaliation against oneself or another and moral justice. In fact, the only moral truth for Camus is the human urge to be dignified. A commitment to human dignity is therefore central to Camus' approach to the question of suicide. That is to say, the originality of Camus resides in his unique response to the basic human inclination towards aberration and violence. His forceful response to those who justify violence, death and violent death—whether inflicted upon the self or upon others—is the argument that he makes in his famous essay, *Neither Victims nor Executioners*:

> All I ask is that, in the midst of a murderous world, we agree to reflect on murder and to make a choice. After that, we can distinguish those who accept the consequences of being murderers themselves or the accomplices of murderers, and those who refuse to dc so with all their force and being. (Camus 2006: 275–276)

It seems that in rejecting violence, Camus is also asking us to reject suicide heroically, in order to be able to make a conscious and deliberate choice, to recognise and appreciate the existential value of human life—life as plurality and as solidarity. Camus' choice of life and human solidarity is exactly the point where the arguments against suicide must be made.

IV POETRY AND SUICIDE
Paul Celan

In the words of George Steiner, Paul Celan 'was a stranger to life' (Steiner 2011: 207). The Romanian-born poet of the German language committed suicide in 1970 by throwing himself into the river Seine in Paris. Paul Celan, originally Paul Antschel, is often regarded as one of the greatest post-war German language poets. The French poet Henri Michaux paid him tribute with a poem entitled '*Le Jour, les Jours, la Fin des Jours*' (The Day, the Days, the End of Days), which ends with the following words:

> I see men motionless
> lying in barges
> Out of here.
> Whatever else, out of here.
> The long knife of the wave will stop the Word.
>
> (Michaux 1997: 236)

Celan's life was certainly stopped by the waves of the river Seine, but not his words. In his numerous poems, they lie on the page as living expressions of death and suffering. 'Death is a master from Germany' is a recurring verse in his poem '*Todesfuge*' (Fugue of Death), which shows us how poetry can be a language of anguish and reminiscence. Considered to be 'the true bard of the Holocaust', Celan's poetry recounts the deaths of Jews in the extermination camps, but it also voices an acute awareness of human survival, of what it means to survive against all odds. Celan was the poet of the living experience of death—of his parents, and later his child—but he was also a poet of the forgotten paths of history, which he tried to remember and to bring back to life through his poems. Above all, he wanted to bear witness to Auschwitz through his poetry. 'To write poetry after Auschwitz is barbaric', declared Theodor Adorno (1983: 34). But Celan wrote poetry on Auschwitz as a survivor, not as a spectator. Because for Celan, poetry was not a spectacle; it was a remembrance of life and its horrors.

> Celan's poetics addresses not only what Adorno conceived as poetry's need to speak the silent language of horror, but (if such qualifications are possible in the face of utter destruction) also the origins of poetry in the realm of its specific linguistic mode—the language of a singular human being. One of the most intriguing steps Celan takes on his way to establishing the poem as a figure of the other addresses concretely the singularity of human beings, the singularity of the language of those most radically marked as others. (Eshel 2004: 65–66)

Celan opposed this *singularity* of human beings in their ways of dying with dignity to the monolithic conception of death exemplified by the mass extermination of millions of men, women and children in the concentration camps. Clearly, death was one of the dominant themes in his poetry. For Celan, there is a close relationship between words and death, as suggests the following elegy he wrote for the death of the French poet, Paul Eluard, in the autumn of 1952: 'Lay in his grave for the dead man the words/ he spoke so as to live' (Celan 2001). About the Paul Eluard elegy, one should know that in 1950 Andre Breton urged Eluard to intercede for the freedom of Zavis Kalandra, a surrealist poet and survivor of Hitler's camps, condemned to death by a Czech Stalinist tribunal. Eluard refused to intervene, and Kalandra was hanged. Because Celan's poems, very often, deal strongly with 'death' and with 'loss' of 'words', 'language', and 'homeland', any effort to separate Celan's suicide from his poetry becomes questionable. This heightened sensibility to death remained with Celan all his life. When he lost his first child in 1953, within days of his birth, he wrote to a friend that the death of his child was 'hard, hard, hard' (Celan, quoted in Felstiner 2001: 72). Everything Celan ever wrote, especially on the Holocaust, was as a witness to death. In a cycle of poems, he wrote the poem, 'In Front of a Candle', where his mother, as a child, points to his own child's death. The poem begins with the lines:

> Of beaten gold,
> as you instructed me, Mother,
> I shaped the candlestick
>
> (Celan 2002: 55)

Celan wrote the poem in the voice of a child-adult. Celan speaks here, once again, the language of singularity in relation to the death of his mother and his son. His argument that poetry is an expression of this singularity points to a poetic path which freezes the wounds of history. Celan's remembrance of death is in fact closely related to his mourning of the past, as the child of a dead mother, and his difficulty in adapting to the world of the living. One could thus say that Celan's poetics is that of the resurrection of the suffering word. Celan's human struggle against death turns into a permanent anguish with the limits of language. This is one reason why he started reading Heidegger, though he knew well about the latter's involvement with Nazism. But as Steiner observes, 'Heidegger's pressure on the limits of language, his innovations within the crucible of violently forged syntax provided Celan with a vital stimulus and "complementarity" (in quantum theory contrary truths may both be true) (Steiner 2011: 208–209).

Living with the echoes of the dead was not easy for Celan. The only way he could protect the word was by keeping vigil at the borders of time. 'Celan's insistence that the poem remains mindful of decisive dates points to the inscription of history, the inscription of memory, in the poem—to the way in which the historical contributes a crucial component in the "conversation"' (Eshel 2004: 64–65). Writing poetry, for Celan, meant listening closely to the past. The act of poetic creation was, for him, an intellectual and philosophical adventure into a Socratic examination of the soul, and an apprenticeship for Death. He recognised that being a poet means living dangerously. The danger is because, in addition to the self, the poet also speaks on behalf of the Other. As Celan argues in his well-known speech 'The Meridian', given on the occasion of receiving the Georg Büchner Prize, on 22 October 1960:

> But the poem speaks. It is mindful of its dates, but it speaks. True, it speaks on its own, its very own behalf. But I think—and this will hardly surprise use—that the poem has always hoped, for this very reason, to speak also on behalf of the strange—no, I can no longer use this word—on behalf of the other, who knows, perhaps of altogether other. (Celan 2006: 48)

Therefore, as a travelling companion of the poem, the poet, too, is on the Socratic path of returning to his soul. Using Heidegger's terminology, Celan speaks of 'the search for ourselves' as an act of 'homecoming':

> Ladies and gentlemen, I find something which consoles me a bit for having walked this impossible road in your presence, this road of the impossible. I find the connective which, like the poem, leads to encounters. I find something as immaterial as

> language, yet earthly, terrestrial, in the shape of a circle which, via both poles, rejoins itself and on the way serenely crosses even the tropics: I find a meridian... (Celan 2006: 55)

And he goes on to ask,

> Is it on such paths that poems take us...? And are these paths only detours...from you to you? But they are, among how many others, the paths on which language becomes voice. They are encounters, paths from a voice to a listening You, natural paths, outlines for existence perhaps, for projecting ourselves into the search for ourselves...A kind of homecoming. (ibid.: 53)

In other words, what Celan is telling us is that encountering the poem is also an act of returning to oneself—it is an encounter with the Otherness of Oneself. Memory is taken away and given back by this encounter, which is but a moment in time. Celan thinks of those who are gone, and he assures us, and himself, that they can be revived and returned to us through poetry. But Celan had no faith in life, because it left him with nothing but memories. He witnessed the horrors of the past through the power of the word, and he relived them. Yet, when confronted by the unspeakable, he remained silent. He could do no more than repeat the words of Moses in Arnold Schoenberg's *Moses und Aron*: 'O Word, thou Word that I lack' (Stuckenschmidt 2011: 347).

As an extension of his life, Celan's suicide, too, was undoubtedly a poetic gesture—a gesture without words. Nonetheless it would be permissible to suppose that Celan's act of suicide, his final poetic statement, was also an effort to voice and to speak the unspeakable where and when words failed. Having discovered the destruction and the ultimate fragility and destructibility of words, which can both distort and be distorted, the poet then had no other recourse but to destroy himself—for a poet is nothing without words. And, as Adorno says, 'only death is an image of undistorted life' (Adorno 2005: 78). Be that as it may, 'Celan and his poetry establish an authentic moral for our time. Celan is the incontrovertible witness, misunderstood even in his death itself, who speaks to us of our immemorial duty: *Yizkor*. Memory' (Suied 1999: 219). Celan's poetry is the poetry of a man whom history has killed in his soul, of a man confronted by the horror of extermination camps. And yet, it seems strange but inevitable that Celan, a survivor of the Holocaust, wrote his poems in German, the language celebrated by the Nazis. His later poems were a mute testimony of the poet's silence with regard to language itself—as if the words were impotent and could no longer express his feverish existential loneliness and anguish. Celan's poetry joins here the theatrical language of Samuel Beckett, another Parisian exile whom he never met. But, as John Felstiner asks, wasn't there always an unspoken understanding between the two? And,

> ...hadn't they been meeting all along, those years in Paris—the older man a more-or-less voluntary Irish exile to France and French, the younger man, orphaned, homelandless, reaching Paris but cleaving to German: Beckett chipping away at silence with 'this dust of words,' Celan with his 'gasping words,' with the 'prayer-sharp knives / of my / silence'? During the 1953 opening run of *En attendant Godot*, where Didi and Gogo go on 'blathering about nothing in particular,' Celan composed 'The Vintagers,' in which 'bent toward blindness and lamed,' a 'latemouth' thirsts for wine, a 'crook stick speaks into / the silence of answers.' (Felstiner 2004: 38)

On 20 April 1970, Celan took a walk along Pont Mirabeau, and drowned himself in the Seine. His body was found seven miles downstream by a French fisherman. Why did he choose to die on 20 April, on Hitler's birthday? Again, as in the case of Mishima and many other writers and poets, much more than an act of despair, Celan's suicide was a way of affirming the vitality and nobility of words and, simultaneously, acknowledging their ultimate and complete failure to articulate all of human experience, and pointing to the tangible but fragile reality of a dark and inarticulate world in which a 'crook stick speaks into / the silence of answers' (Felstiner 2004: 38). Celan's suicide is a reminder of a passage of Beckett's novel *L'Innommable* (The Unnamable): 'And yet I am afraid, afraid of what my words will do to me, to my refuge, yet again...If I could speak and yet say nothing, really nothing? Then I might escape being gnawed to death' (Beckett 2009: 297).

Celan's suicide was not spectacular like that of Yukio Mishima. No spectators, no cameras were present. And yet, they both committed suicide the same year. However, what remains an enigma in Celan's case is that no one in his entourage had anticipated it. Perhaps Celan had tried, before his tragic decision, to find a last refuge in poetry, and perhaps the stubbornly closed door of words seemed to him to be the ultimate symbol of his tragic existential situation. Little by little, words had turned into silence. He had no way out of his memories, no recourse to a future. Even his death took place in the dark, alone on a bridge and with a minimum of noise and embarrassment. It was the suicide of a poet alone with his words. But much of the unease felt at Paul Celan's suicide is perhaps also due to the fact that poets like him find it difficult to survive in a world devoid of *transcendence*. As Steiner gravely notes:

> A civilization without the possibility of transcendence—what Nietzsche calls the *mysterium tremendum* of man, what Heidegger (with caution) attempts to formulate—a civilization in which we

> can no longer say, like Wittgenstein, 'If I could have, I would have dedicated my philosophical inquiries to God,' a civilization that has lost those possibilities is certainly...in serious danger. (Steiner and Adler 2017: 73)

Celan's suicide was no accident. Neither was it an accident of history, like the death of Spanish poet Federico Garcia Lorca. Celan had accepted his suicide and he was ready for it. He left life quickly and with elegance, hoping that someone will recite the *Kaddish* for him. Celan lived as a Jew, and he died as a Jew, refusing to allow language to suffer from his very own human pains. The horror of that thought is inconceivable for a poet who lives with, by and through words. 'What is a poet?' asked the great Danish philosopher Kierkegaard: 'An unhappy man who hides deep anguish in his heart', he replied (Kierkegaard 2009: 16). Celan carried with him this poetic anguish, while he continued to write poetry and to teach German literature at the École Normale Supérieure. During all this time, as his poetry reveals, Celan was in constant search of transcendence and deliverance—both from his past and from his status as a Holocaust survivor and exile. Through his poems, he quite clearly demonstrates the distance he puts between his poetic art and craft, and everyday usage and principles of language. Though 'suicide' had never been at the centre of his poetic examination of life, it is evident that Celan succeeded in delivering his poetry from the customary moral burden borne by much of European history.

This reminds us of a passage of Honoré de Balzac's novel *La Peau de Chagrin* (The Wild Ass's Skin), which was printed in the *Revue de Paris* in 1831 under the title *Le Suicide d'un Poète* (The Suicide of a Poet). Balzac memorably wrote:

> There is something noble as well as terrible about suicide....when a great man breaks, he has soared up to the heavens, espied some inaccessible paradise,

> and then fallen from a great height....How many young talents confined to an attic room wither and perish for lack of a friend, a consoling wife, alone in the midst of a million fellow humans...God alone understands the chaos of ideas, the abandoned poems, the despair or stifled cries for help, the vain attempts, the masterpieces begun but not finished. Every suicide is a sublime poem of melancholy. (Balzac 2012: 9)

More than an act of despair, Balzac considered suicide to be a heroic act. The nineteenth-century idealisation of suicide by authors like Balzac can also be traced in French modernist painters like Édouard Manet. As Ulrike Ilg observes, in his famous painting *Le Suicidé*, Manet 'liberates' suicide in two fundamentally important aspects:

> First of all, he does not give a moral lesson, and does not...represent suicide as a melodramatic incident or...shape it as an accusation against present social conditions. Secondly he refuses to assume the role of a narrator: He omits nearly all indication that could explain the circumstances of the action and makes sure that its protagonist remains completely anonymous to us, depicting the upper part of the suicide's body in such an extremely oblique perspective that his facial traits remain very indistinct. By this consequent de-historicization and non-narration, *Le Suicidé* assumes a programmatic character. (Ilg 2002: 187)

Taking into account Manet's painting, one can say that though Celan is not a poet of suicide, he is certainly *Le Suicidé* of poetry. Celan's suicide was left to us by no testament. He died alone, and his body was caught seven miles downstream by a fisherman who had no idea that he was fishing out a famous poet. Like in Manet's painting, Celan's suicide was devoid of a narrative. But there was a history behind it, accompanied by a vision of death. The value of Celan's poetry is most apparent when brought close to the historical reality and the singularity of his sufferings as a Holocaust survivor. For Celan, poetry was not simply there—it had to become 'real' (*Wirklich*). Because, according to him, 'Reality for poems is in no way something that stands established, already given, but something standing in question, that's to be put in question. In a poem, what's real happens...The poem itself, insofar as it is a real poem, is aware of the questionableness of its own beginning' (Felstiner 2001: 118). But Celan also knew, better than anyone, that this 'homecoming' of words was not a full return to reality. Everywhere in Celan's poetry there is a questioning of the relationship of words and reality, and of the limits of language in its ability to encompass human experience and emotion. One can sense in Celan's questioning the impossibility of narrating the concrete details of a specific event, like the death of his mother. Celan's 'desperate conversation' with reality is accompanied by an unspeakable sense of loss.

> Celan's most acute loss was the loss of his mother. This most important, structuring moment in Celan's biography—the moment in which love didn't work out—is accompanied by a profound sense of guilt. Indeed, there is some suggestion that Celan felt himself to be an agent in his mother's disappearance, or, at the very least, that he acknowledged a connection between his choices and her death. In the end, it was impossible for Celan to narrate the concrete details of her disappearance... (Klink 2000: 11)

Celan found history insurmountable. Perhaps that is why he tried to transcend it by committing suicide. He wanted to get off the train of history. But his poetry reminds us that what makes words meaningful are the individual human lives behind it. A poet is someone who values the immediacy of actual lived lives over and beyond recorded history.

> Poetry, Celan reminds us, has ontology in it; poetic languages hold out the possibility of reintroducing the ground of being...A poem holds out a common world. In this way, poetry reconstructs the relation between an actual, particular life and the general life, between the world of appearances and what lends meaning to those appearances, between experience and holiness, between what comes to pass and what is most valuable. In poetry, in Celan's poetry, separate and provisional selves are summoned out of their personal lives into the ground of that life. (Klink 2000: 17)

Celan was a true poet in what he saw better and further than his contemporaries. He foresaw the misfortunes of humanity to which the vices of history had led us and he sounded the cry of alarm in his poetry. In that sense, he was very close to Simone Weil, who wrote:

> Affliction...is hideous as life in its nakedness always is, like an amputated stump, like the swarming of insects. Life without form. Survival is then the only attachment....when all other attachments are replaced by that of survival...Quasi-hell on earth.... Human injustice as a general rule produces not martyrs but quasi-damned souls. Beings who have fallen into this quasi-hell are like someone stripped and wounded by robbers. They have lost the clothing of character. The greatest suffering which allows any of a man's roots to remain is at an infinite distance from this quasi-hell. (Weil 2005: 101)

With his instinctive sensitivity, his empathy for genuine suffering, and a soul entirely preoccupied by the beautiful and the true, Celan, knew how to stand in the world as a survivor and how to rise above the necessity of history. As Steiner puts it, 'For Celan stars had gone yellow in remembrance of the horrors inflicted on those condemned to wear them' (Steiner 2011: 209). His suicidal gaze was an act of contempt for those who found beauty and truth in everything, including in the synonym of life. But as Celan argues in his Meridian speech: 'The poem is the place where the synonym becomes impossible: it has only its own plane of language and significance. Emerging out of language, the poem steps over against language. This over against cannot be sublated' (Celan 1999: 104, quoted in Müller-Sievers 2004: 146). Perhaps it would be correct to apply Celan's mode of thinking to his own suicide, by trying to understand it as 'a step over against life'. Is it not true that suicide is an exhaustion of language and a desperate desire to transcend life? It indicates how Celan may have developed his vision of death and loss as the 'unspeakable', which in the end was to culminate in his own suicide.

By drowning himself in the Seine, Celan took another step in a direction he had already explored through the deaths of his parents and his child. His memories as a survivor were anchored in time. Perhaps if he had written on suicide, it is possible that he might have been able to overcome his profound and inarticulate grief over their deaths, his loneliness, and, subsequently, his suicide. 'For dead are the angels and blind was the Lord in the region of Akra, and there is no one who might tend for me in sleep those who went to their rest here' (Celan, quoted in Stern 1983: 7). As an abandoned survivor of the war, and with no prospect of returning to his homeland, Celan was always carrying within himself the last minutes of his life. His heroic combat with death was destined to collapse into an act committed in absolute isolation. Destiny was for him like a message in a bottle—always accompanied by the hope of being discovered by someone. This was the essence of poetry and language for Celan, which he conveyed to his audience in the speech he delivered in 1958 on the 'Occasion of Receiving the Literature Prize of the Free Hanseatic City of Bremen':

> Within reach, close and not lost, there remained... this one thing: language...But it had to pass through its own answerlessnesses...through the thousand darknesses of death-bringing speech....In this language I have sought...to write...to speak...to explore where I was...to sketch out reality for myself...a poem is not timeless...A poem...can be a message in a bottle, sent out in the (not always greatly hopeful) belief that it may...sometime wash up on land...These are the efforts of someone...shelterless...who goes with his very being to language, stricken by and seeking reality. (Celan, quoted in Felstiner 1982: 23)

Celan's suicide was a sacrifice of the poet for the sake of poetry. It was a way for him to show that he was engaged with words until the very end. He surrendered himself to oblivion for the sake of the remembrance of others. It was this overwhelming concern for human forgetfulness which took Celan out of life. He preferred suicide to political partisanship. Unlike poets such as Mayakovski, Eluard, Aragon and Neruda, Celan did not want to be a militant; he wanted to be a poet who could help humanity remember its past. Throughout his life, he presented himself as someone who reminded us of the Shoah, which happened, and which should not have happened. The Holocaust stirred up a flood of emotions in Celan that he never could overcome or forget. The anguish of this horrific experience haunted him until the end of his life. Though, seduced by the magical power and beauty of words, Celan always returned to the intellectual source of the Holocaust, the German language, and attempted to understand the myriad intersections of language and history.

> Celan's poems seek to embody a destroyed heritage. Celan seeks to greet the Other whom occidental discourse had wanted to colonize or convert or gas depending on the century and the urgencies of the absurd search for a scapegoat. Celan underlines

> the necessity of the Word in human relations, the truth of sharing in a world that chose schizophrenia and the demonization of the Similar. (Suied 1999: 218)

Let us not forget that it was Celan who provided the German translation of Jean Cayrol's text, which was used by Alain Resnais for his documentary on the Holocaust: *Nuit et Brouillard*. Resnais' film takes this thermodynamics of horror apart and seems to tell us: 'Watch out! Look where it starts!'. For Adorno, the horror started with our indifference to the slaughterhouse of animals. For Celan, it started with the use of the German language. Human herds were brought to the slaughterhouse, their bodies were reduced to ashes, and they called it '*Arbeit Macht Frei*' (Work Sets You Free). Celan's poetry looked straight at the distress of those millions of innocents and asked the question: What can we do here today that this does not happen again? Celan warned us that language can itself become a thermodynamics of horror when he wrote:

> Whichever stone you lift—
> you lay bare
> those who need the protection of stones...
> Whichever word you speak—
> you owe
> to destruction
>
> (Celan, quoted in Felstiner 2001: 71)

Traces in Celan's poetry manifest a lifelong preoccupation with the destruction of language, the destruction of meaning, and with what is forgotten. Celan inscribed himself within a tradition of German poets and, among them, Hölderlin in particular. He pointed to the spiritual presence of Hölderlin in his poems. Like Hölderlin, he knew that 'memory is taken and given by the sea' (Celan, quoted in Felstiner 2001: 76), but he also knew that to retrieve memory was 'a poetic dwelling upon the earth' (ibid.). Hölderlin came to signify for Celan one who had realised the fusion of poetic dwelling and the German language—a fusion whose ultimate chapter was Hölderlin's madness and Celan's suicide—and an enigma that, in Steiner's words, only 'language as the definite nucleus of being' could unravel (Steiner 2011: 214).

V THE AESTHETICS OF SUICIDE

Yukio Mishima

When he committed suicide by seppuku at the age of forty-five on 25 November 1970, Yukio Mishima was recognised in his country and abroad as the greatest writer of post-war Japan. His dramatically staged suicide was preceded by a speech in which he addressed the Jieitai soldiers from the balcony at Eastern Army Headquarters in Tokyo. A talented writer, a husband, a father, a homosexual, an actor in Japanese gangster movies and in his own productions, the head of a private army of young soldiers who was obsessed with bodybuilding and the samurai code, and finally a contender for the Nobel Prize in Literature, Mishima remains a fascinating and largely misunderstood character. Unlike Celan and many writers and poets who committed suicide without writing about this subject, Mishima started meditating about ritual self-killing in the 1950s. One can clearly trace the presence of death next to that of beauty in many of Mishima's writings. The cult of the masculine body glorified and strengthened by the samurai sword and the heroic blood of the martyr became dominant symbols of Mishima's aesthetic code and artistic life. In the same manner, Mishima posed as San Sebastian, a Christian martyr whose body was pierced by arrows, for a Japanese photographer and played the role of an army officer who committed seppuku, in his own film entitled *Patriotism*. The film was based on a short story of the same title written by Mishima in the autumn of 1960, ten years before his suicide, describing the last hours of Lieutenant Shinji Takeyama and his young bride Reiko, who commit a double suicide. Mishima sketched in his story the ceremonial disembowelment of the young lieutenant in detail.

> By the time the lieutenant had at last drawn the sword across to the right side of his stomach, the blade was already cutting shallow and had revealed its naked tip, slippery with blood and grease. But, suddenly stricken by a fit of vomiting, the lieutenant cried out...the stomach...now abruptly heaved...and the entrails burst through...[they]...gave an impression of...almost disagreeable vitality...A raw smell filled the room....It would be difficult to imagine a more heroic sight than that of the lieutenant at this moment, as he mustered his strength and flung back his head. (Mishima 1966: 114–115)

For Mishima, suicide was both an aesthetic and a heroic act. He considered true beauty a sensuous expression of death. Although beauty and death may seem disparate, even contradictory, concepts to some, in Mishima's sublimely seductive language, death becomes not just beautiful but erotic and sensual. In his book *Sun and Steel* he observes:

> The moment of death, the moment when, even without being seen, the fiction of being seen and the beauty of the object are permitted. Of such is the beauty of the suicide squad, which is recognized as beauty not only in the spiritual sense but, by men in general, in an ultra erotic sense also. (Mishima 1970b: 55)

Identifying himself with his tragic heroes, Mishima, through his words and his actions in life, transformed samurai suicide into a noble mode of death and the heroic act *par excellence*. However, unlike the others mentioned previously, Mishima approached the idea and the act of suicide as the end result of a shared suffering in a brotherhood of warriors, where the individual had to be sublimated and sacrificed for the sake of the group. As he explained:

> Only through the group, I realized—through sharing the suffering of the group—could the body reach that height of existence that the individual alone could never attain. And for the body to reach that level at which the divine might be glimpsed, a dissolution of the individual was necessary. The tragic quality of the group was also necessary—the quality that constantly raised the group out of the abandon and torpor into which it was prone to lapse, leading it on to ever-mounting shared suffering, and so to death—which meant, of course, that it must be a community of warriors... (Mishima 1970b: 87)

Mishima's creation of the 'Tatenokai' or Shield Society in 1966, with the purpose of defending the Emperor of Japan against the attacks of the Left, turned out to be more of a personal and romantic quest for an exemplary and heroic death, rather than a political and military adventure. Mishima's involvement with the Tatenokai until the final moments of his life was a way for him to transcend the more distanced and mediated acts of thinking and writing through the pure, unmediated reality and immediacy of action. In other words, Mishima needed extreme and violent action in order to be able to confront the violence of death. It was only by conquering the domain of life and action that he could surmount his fear of death and dying like a samurai. That is why, for years, he prepared and trained his body through intensive physical exercise, to ready himself for the ultimate moment of the unveiling of death. He argued:

> I cherished a romantic impulse toward death, yet at the same time I required a strictly classical body as its vehicle; a peculiar sense of destiny made me believe that the reason why my romantic impulse toward death remained unfulfilled...was the immensely simple fact that I lacked the necessary physical qualifications. A powerful, tragic frame and sculpturesque muscles were indispensable in a romantically noble death. Any confrontation between weak, flabby flesh and death seemed to me absurdly inappropriate....And it deeply offended my romantic pride that it should be this unsuitability that had permitted me to survive the war. (Mishima 1970b: 27–28)

Mishima had planned his suicide for months, if not years. His acute awareness of his body, as also expressed in his strenuous exercises and participation in the rigorous training of the Self-Defense Force, was a way for him to find a harmonious balance between the power of creativity and the strength of physicality. Unsurprisingly, all of Mishima's creative work finds its true meaning in the epiphany of his suicide.

> While Mishima's suicide can be seen as the culmination of his life project—the final step in his unification of 'action and art'—it is also the case that it was this very act that brought his creative life to a close forever. In eradicating the nihilistic gap between his real life and the ideal for which he longed, Mishima also decisively obliterated his future potential. (Marmysz 2017: 179)

Mishima made the journey, from a man of words to a man of swords, through his own body. In this process, he obscured the line between the writer and the samurai. For Mishima, the synthesis between the Japanese philosophy of Bushido and the Greek idealisation of physical beauty was only possible in the heroic art of dying. He realised that his quest for the purity and sublimation of the self could only be glorified through an act of seppuku. 'In Mishima, Apollo finally triumphed over Dionysus. For the man himself, perhaps the mental and spiritual conviction he achieved was worthwhile, bringing a sense of completion and climax to his life story; a conclusion that helped to shape and make sense of everything he had experienced up to that point' (Marmysz 2017: 201). By dying honourably in the manner of a Japanese warrior, Mishima tried to bring his ritual suicide in line with his aesthetic vision of reality. He preferred the dramatic and heroic death of a beautiful, perfectly sculpted, powerful body to the slow death of an ageing, diseased and decaying body of a man who could live for decades. Mishima's deep despair at the certain future disintegration of his masculine body due to age was twinned with his despair at the gradual decline of the majesty and power of imperial Japan. He chose to put an end to this despair by publicly thrusting a sword into his stomach.

On the fatal morning of November 1970, Mishima had submitted the last portion of the fourth and final volume of his tetralogy of novels, *The Sea of Fertility*. As Hisaaki Yamanouchi notes:

> The completion of that work meant the breaking of the delicate balance between the created world of his work and commitment to life. He had to confront the freedom to choose....If Mishima had remained the type of writer who...felt handicapped in life but compensated for it by creating his work, he would have kept on living in that mode. Now he had acquired physical strength, by means of which he could extinguish his own body so that his soul could live. It was a paradox of attaining the fullness of life through death. (Yamanouchi 1972: 13)

Mishima's fascination with suicide had not only a romantic essence, but also an erotic framework. This is a reminder of Mishima's adolescence, portrayed in his confessional work, *The Confessions of a Mask*, where he underlined his differences with Japanese boys of his age. Comparing himself with the other boys in the act of masturbation, Mishima observed, 'In my state of autohypnosis I overlooked the fact that, in spite of the identical nature of the physical action, there was a profound difference so far as its mental objects were concerned' (Nathan 1975: 25). The young Mishima did not masturbate with images of naked women, but with that of St. Sebastian, a dying martyr with a pierced body. As he recounts his first time,

> That day, the instant I looked upon the picture, my entire being trembled with some pagan joy. My blood soared up; my loins swelled as though in wrath. The monstrous part of me that was on the point of bursting awaited my use of it with unprecedented ardor, upbraiding me for my ignorance, panting indignantly. My hands, completely unconsciously, began a motion they had never been taught. I felt a secret, radiant something rise swift-footed to the attack from inside me. Suddenly it burst forth, bringing with it a blinding intoxication. ...This was my first ejaculation. (Mishima 1963: 40–41)

Later in life, Mishima chose the eroticism of death because the eroticism of art brought him only temporary satisfaction, or at least because it didn't bring together life and death. Mishima's 'language of eroticism tries to bridge the gap between the sexual body and language by taking squarely as a narrative issue the paradox of the desiring subject's violent reaction to beauty, then mediating this reaction through the structure of transgression and betrayal' (Wallace 1997: 199). It seems that Mishima's strong phantasm with words and images had a limit in life. It's the steel that gave him a heroic consciousness and a tragic sensitivity. The symbolism of the samurai sword was related immediately to that of blood and death. According to Henry Scott-Stokes,

> Blood gave him [Mishima] a sexual thrill—this was one of his most important 'confessions' and the core of his aesthetics. The beauty of the spilt blood of the samurai has been endlessly poeticized by the Japanese, who liken the short-lived blossom of the cherry tree to the life of the samurai. Mishima, however, romanticized death and blood in a manner foreign to the Japanese classical tradition. (Scott-Stokes 1974: 83)

Not many people knew or could have imagined that Mishima would actually cross the line between the depiction and the performance of seppuku in his writings or acting and the actual act. The reason is simple. By following beauty in death, Mishima the artist seamlessly became Mishima the samurai. But, like some of the characters in his novels, he could not apprehend or experience the beauty of death without confronting the act of seppuku face to face.

> Only in that final moment would he know, for himself, if his action was beautiful and heroic enough, i.e. tragic enough, to nullify the distinction between art and action. It all depended on how much 'physical courage' he would be able to summon. It may be deemed significant in this respect, that the execution of his seppuku was as flawless as his revolt had been ridiculous. But in any case, his courage in the strict sense of the word cannot be doubted, as it is evident that he dared submit himself to fate. (Abelsen 1996: 679)

Mishima's fascination with death was born at a young age. An acute Mishima reader may be able to sense that his fate was already present in the very first words that he wrote. Mishima never thought or wrote about death in a simple and ordinary manner. For him, death always had a sacrificial dimension. Like for his protagonist, Mizoguchi, in *Kinkakuji* (1956) or *The Temple of the Golden Pavilion* (1959), the intense desire for immortality created an anguish in Mishima which forced him to destroy that which he prized most—his beautiful body—in the same way that Mizoguchi came to realise 'that it is only through destruction of the physical manifestation of the Temple that its essence can be liberated and finally achieve immortality' (Marmysz 2017: 186). Here, for Mishima, the 'temple' is also his own perfect, powerful body. His suicide is the culmination and completion of the staging of the figure of the writer-actor-samurai by Mishima himself. As Margarite Yourcenar notes:

> Let us remember that the central reality must be sought in the writer's work: it is what the writer chose to write, or was compelled to write, that finally matters. And certainly Mishima's carefully premeditated death is part of his work. However, while a film such as 'Patriotism,' or a passage such as the description of Isao's suicide in 'Runaway Horses,' sheds light on the writer's end and partly explains it, the author's death, at most, grants these works authenticity but does nothing to elucidate them. (Yourcenar 1986: 1)

As premeditated as Mishima's suicide was, it was nevertheless the conclusion of a life lived through many trials and tribulations. It came to an end with Mishima's final work and masterpiece, *The Sea of Fertility*. It is interesting that the title of this tetralogy refers to a plain occupying the centre of the moon, which is nothing but a vast arid desert.

> On the morning of his death Mishima left the final volume of *The Sea of Fertility Tetralogy* with his maid, giving instructions for its delivery to the publisher. This final volume was the culmination of a four-book

> cycle of novels consisting of *Spring Snow, Runaway Horses, The Temple of Dawn* and *The Decay of the Angel*. This series tells the story of the (apparent) reincarnation of a single soul in four different people who are fated to die tragic, youthful deaths. The various incarnations of this soul are witnessed by Honda, a Japanese lawyer who is the story's central character. (Marmysz 2017: 199)

With masterful and deliberate aesthetic precision, Mishima chose to hand over his last manuscript to his publisher an hour before his death on 25 November 1970—a date printed on the last page of his novel. Mishima's suicide note read: 'Human life is limited, but I want to live forever' (Ross 2006: 55). Arriving at the headquarters of the Japanese Defense Forces with four chosen members of the Shield Society, and after taking the commander of the garrison hostage in his office, Mishima gave a speech for the Self-Defense Force (SDF) in which he exhorted them to take action against the Constitution imposed upon them and return to the pre-war spiritual values of Japan. Alluding to the Non-proliferation Treaty (NPT), which was negotiated only eight months earlier between Japan and the Western powers, Mishima, in 'his ultranationalist appeal', argued:

> Where is the samurai's soul? Where are you, a colossal arsenal without soul, going? ... since the NPT was related to the grand strategy for the nation and it was obviously the reproduction of the prewar unequal treaty (with Britain and the U.S.), there appeared no SDF general who committed ritual suicide as protest. (Funatsu 2001)

Mishima's moral and aesthetic preoccupation with samurai values and the samurai code of life and death go back to his publication of an introduction to *Hagakure* (translated variously as 'In the Shadow of Leaves' or 'Hidden by the

Leaves'), a book by Yamamoto Tsunetomo which offers advice on how to transcend the monotony of everyday life and provides a set of rules to guide the reader to a greater nobility of spirit. Tsunetomo recommended the following:

> Consequently, if someone were to ask, 'What is the true meaning of the Way of the Samurai?' the person who would be able to answer promptly is rare. This is because it has not been established in one's mind beforehand. ...The Way of the Samurai is found in death. ...It is not particularly difficult. Be determined and advance. To say that dying without reaching one's aim is to die a dog's death is the frivolous way of sophisticates. When pressed with the choice of life or death, it is not necessary to gain one's aim. (Tsunetomo, quoted in Hubbard 2016: 139)

In his commentary on *Hagakure*, Mishima affirmed the sayings of Tsunetomo. He wrote: 'I discovered that the way of the samurai is death. In a life or death crisis, simply settle it by choosing immediate death' (Mishima 1979: 89). This simple, calm and untroubled acceptance of death as the most obvious and categorical choice is one of the main principles of the *Hagakure*. This noble death concerns not only the samurai himself, but also his immediate entourage and family. For example, in the famous legend of the forty-seven *ronin* (in feudal Japan, a ronin was a wandering samurai without a master or lord), the mother of a samurai chooses to cut her throat the night before her son leaves for war. Mishima aspired to attain this same nobility of spirit. The samurai code lived within him, and through it he tried to reconcile his ethics with his aesthetics and his art. We can find the seed of Mishima's seppuku in his celebration and care of a strong, beautiful body, right until the moment of its destruction. Mishima's aesthetic approach to the male body, and specifically to his own muscular flesh, is very similar to the representation of the

Golden Temple by Mizoguchi, the protagonist of Mishima's 1956 novel *Kinkakuji* (*The Temple of the Golden Pavilion*), earlier mentioned.

> Mishima considers his hero Mizoguchi to be a victim of this evil world that has lost its traditional moral center, and this loss accounts for the desperation of the young man's action...When Mizoguchi actually travels to see the temple, however, he feels betrayed, and it is not until his return to the provinces that an awareness of its beauty revives within him....in his mind: the temple seems most beautiful when it is absent. The seed of Mizoguchi's compulsion to destroy or deface beauty is planted here....His simultaneous idolization of beauty and wish for its destruction foreshadow the burning of Kinkakuji. (Nemoto 1993: 233–234)

For Mishima, the idealisation of Bushido, the samurai code of thinking and being, went hand in hand with his glorification of pre-war Japan, with the Japanese emperor as a deity at its centre. Mishima's inextricably entwined and simultaneous love and hatred for Japanese culture reflect his ambivalent feelings about his own body—as an artist and as a samurai. His nostalgic yearning for the golden, invincible Japan of the samurais is present in all his modes of being: writing, acting, speaking and dying. Mishima's portrayal of a modern Japan which cannot celebrate and perpetuate its glorious past is a confession which turns into an obsession for self-destruction. He decided to fight a timeless battle to join eternity. As he underlines in *Sun and Steel*:

> That which lurked beyond the flash of the fist and the stroke of the fencing sword was at the opposite pole from verbal expression—that much, at least, was apparent from the feeling it conveyed...Beyond the fist, beyond the tip of the bamboo sword, a new

> reality had reared its head, a reality that rejected all expression of phenomena by resort to abstractions. ...The opponent and I dwelt in the same world [facing each other] without any intermediary imagination, both belonging to the same world of action and strength—the world, that is, of 'being seen'. (Mishima 1970a: 34)

In his life and in his death, Mishima wanted to be *seen*. For him, 'being' was 'appearing'—to others as well as to himself. His so called 'exhibitionism' was nothing but an act of moving with different characters through a world of appearances. Mishima wanted to be seen, acknowledged, recognised and responded to, as a writer, artiste, actor, body-builder, samurai warrior. All his life, Mishima saw others as spectators of his appearance on the stage of the world. Everything that he did, including his suicide, was staged and meant to be seen by somebody. In fact, Mishima could well have been a Shakespearean actor, personifying Hamlet or Macbeth. If Mishima searched for a mode of transcendence through his art, it was because he was trying to identify and align his ideological and psychological needs with the illusions of the stage in theatre. He found ways of reinstating his idealised Japan in the fictitious structures of stage acting and film making. Even his 'sympathy for the assassins did not become apparent until much later on. Perhaps his sympathy for them did not stem from his political sentiments but from his obsession with death, evident in many other works he wrote' (Melanowicz 1992: 6). Mishima's journey beyond the eternality and fragility of beauty was a way of fulfilling the necessities of death. One can hear the overtones of death both in Mishima's writing and acting. He is constantly searching for the 'Way of the Sword', the pure action, beyond the 'Way of Beauty'. Moreover, Mishima saw

> the aesthetic spirit as an insufficient haven for human repose, as unequal to the task of coping with the

> rigors of real life. At least two corollaries emerge from his view. First, isolating oneself within the dream-like realm of art can lead to loss of rational contact with real life and a consequent growth of anxiety, unhappiness, obsession, madness, and even death. Second, the once-exalted position of the artist in society must now be considered as one enfeebled position among many. (Gillespie 1982: 38)

Mishima was acutely conscious of the weak and fragile position of the artist in post-war Japan. He thus chose the 'Way of the Sword' for its physically tangible confrontation with real life and as an open door to immortality. There is not a shadow of doubt that Mishima is one of the greatest writers in post-war Japan. Yet, he is remembered and celebrated by the Japanese and people around the world more as the author who committed suicide by *harakiri* on 25 November 1970 in front of a shocked crowd, not so much for his written works. Mishima's ritual death made a sensation in the newspapers worldwide, while his death as a novelist was only mourned by those who considered him a great writer. Mishima wanted to live, be known and remembered both as a man of ideas and a man of action. For him, suicide, as understood in the Western notion of it, was an expression of weakness, associated with cowardice and defeatism. Harakiri, on the other hand, was a courageous and noble act that corresponded to a certain notion of human dignity. For this reason, for him death was also closely linked to an ethical sense of duty and values.

Perhaps the most characteristic feature of Mishima's sensibility in life was not hedonistic pleasure, but a melancholy acceptance of life's ephemerality and fragility, which was inseparable from its beauty. For him, the art of dying was simply a matter of knowing when and how to give up life when the moment of death arrives, and embracing that moment. One cannot deny that even in death, he had a peculiar sense of punctuality, of a being in Time. 'Mishima's textualization of death in his writing, no less than the honing of his body through disciplined exercise, is, as it were, authenticated by the obsessive punctuality of his life and death, a punctuality testified to by his manuscripts and letters...' (Wolfe 2014: 37). It is possible therefore to read Mishima's ritualistic suicide as the climactic completion of a life lived as a harmonic symphony.

Mishima's samurai gesture in death turned into a historic Japanese moment exemplified by the exercise of a sovereign will. But his suicide becomes truly interesting only when seen against the backdrop of other famous suicides in the history of humankind. Whether spectacular, dramatic and public like Mishima's or invisible, silent and singular like Celan's, suicide is a fundamental human truth and an experience of *being in the world*. Rather than an act of 'insanity' or 'irrationality' or despair, suicide should also be approached as the age-old human quest for immortality, and furthermore, as the quest for meaning itself.

VI CONCLUSION

The Pursuit of Unhappiness

We are no more at the time of Seneca or Mishima. Suicide has become commonplace in our world. No moral shadows darken suicide. Killing oneself is no more a sin, nor a pathological act. We are no longer even on Durkheim's court, where suicide is an act of hyper-individualism. Social, economic or psychological factors may reinforce an individual's decision to commit suicide, but the final decision remains with the person. However, unlike the common belief, a suicide attempt is not an indication that something is gravely wrong in a person's life. As we saw in some of the previous examples, especially in the case of writers, poets and philosophers, suicide is not supposed to be a 'permanent solution' to a 'temporary problem'. Not everyone commits suicide to escape a problem. Every person lives his or her own manner of suicide. A writer like Stefan Zweig may succumb to despair and take his own life when he finds himself forced into exile. Another artist-writer like Mishima may commit seppuku to experience the absolute beauty and ecstasy of a samurai death, before growing old and witnessing his body decay and diminish with time, and he may do it publicly to make a statement of his death. It would therefore also be wrong to consider suicide to be always a private and solitary act. As we can see in Jacques-Louis David's painting, *The Death of Socrates*, drinking the cup of hemlock was not a private act of suicide for Socrates. In contrast, however, 'Zweig strove all his life, against the demands of fame, loves, and friendships, to preserve his innermost privacy' (Prater 1982: 327).

Stefan Zweig and his wife Lotte committed suicide in February of 1942 by taking an overdose of sleeping pills. At the time, the couple were living in Brazil, where they were received warmly in the beginning, but later kept at a distance because of the strong anti-Semitism of the country's ruler, the dictator Getúlio Vargas. Far from his humanist Europe, with his friends being killed by the Nazis one by one, Zweig felt deeply anguished, alienated and lonely. After having lived 'a life in which intellectual labor meant the purest joy and personal freedom the highest good on earth' (Zweig, quoted in Prochnik 2017), for Zweig, suicide was a way to exit the stage with dignity.

Some other German-speaking exiles, who also fled Germany to escape persecution after the rise of Nazism, regarded Zweig's suicide to be a selfish act as they believed that he could have been a great inspiration for a strong moral and spiritual resistance against the Nazis. 'Was he not conscious of any responsibility', wrote Thomas Mann just after Zweig's death, 'toward his many brothers in destiny the world over, for whom the bread of exile is so much harder than it was for him, who was celebrated and free of material cares? Did he regard his life as his own private affair, and simply say: "I suffer too much. Look. I must go"?' (Mann 1963: 281, quoted in Prater 1982: 327). Unlike, Mann, Zweig had lived all his life with the grand idea of an inclusive, pluralist, humanist Europe—that he called his 'spiritual homeland'—which collapsed under the boots of Nazism. He saw the Jews as having played a vital and great role in the rise of high culture in Europe. He also saw himself as a typically assimilated Jew in Austria, and wrote in his memorable autobiography, *The World of Yesterday*, that the Austrian Jews

> felt that their being Austrian was a mission to the world...much, if not the most of all that Europe and America admire today as an expression of a new, rejuvenated Austrian culture, in literature, the theatre, in the arts and crafts, was created by the Viennese Jews, who, in turn, by this manifestation achieved the highest artistic performance of their millennial spiritual activity. (Zweig 1943: 29)

Few readers of his autobiography could really understand what a Europhilic Jew like Stefan Zweig would have felt when the Nazi leaders marched through Vienna after the Anschluss. Zweig's deep pessimism was reinforced by his despair and anger to see how the Jews of Europe were abandoned by everyone and slaughtered like cattle by the Nazis and their allies. *The World of Yesterday* was finished shortly before Zweig's suicide and published after his death. Zweig's suicide note was found by the Brazilian police officers in Petropolis, and translated from the German by Fritz Weil, a German-Jewish manufacturer, who after the Second World War bought the letter and donated it to the National Library of Israel. Zweig wrote the following:

> I would not have asked to rebuild my life in any other place after the world of my own language sank and was lost to me and my spiritual homeland, Europe, destroyed itself. But to start everything anew after a man's 60th year requires special powers, and my own power has been expended after years of wandering homeless. I thus prefer to end my life at the right time, upright, as a man for whom cultural work has always been his purest happiness and personal freedom—the most precious of possessions on this earth. I send greetings to all of my friends: May they live to see the

> dawn after this long night. I, who am most impatient, go before them. (Zweig 1942)

What Zweig shares with us in his suicide note is a feeling of exhaustion, both physical and emotional, by the long years of homeless wandering, and reminds the reader of his 'homesickness' (*Heimweh*) for Europe as his 'spiritual homeland'. But Zweig knew well that the glorious days of the past were gone and that Nazi barbarism had taken over the European '*humanitas*'. He wrote in 1938: 'We are too Erasmian... to prevail against these men who have a battering ram in place of forehead and brain. Against those possessed by the mania of nationalism only those themselves possessed can stand: we are poisoned by our humanity' (Prater 1972: 270). Zweig did not consider himself a vanquished European Jew, but his suicide is certainly a sign of his deep disillusionment with the turning point of European culture. Consequently, one of the most important aspects of Zweig's life and writings was to stress the moral force of culture against barbarity. Being in exile and cut off from books was a terrible deprivation for Zweig. Added to that, 'there was the sadness at the loss of his major public in Germany, at the lack of contact with his remaining friends, and at the deprivation of the active intellectual intercourse which meant so much to him' (Daviau 1959: 11). For Zweig, suicide was the last resort to nobility and culture, and to the 'examined life'. It was an act of moral courage, especially in his situation, as a victim of the absolute dehumanisation of humanitas. Thus, as may be read in his last words:

> his suicide can in no way be construed as a fearful running away from life, as a negative step, but was rather the joyful advance of a man taking positive action. Zweig was determined never to let the reins of his life slip from his hands, as can be seen by his parting message to the world. (Daviau 1959: 11)

In the case of Zweig, suicide was a human imperative, not a subject for intellectual analysis. For individuals like Stefan Zweig, Walter Benjamin and Paul Celan, and even Yukio Mishima (in a different context), suicide was a way of transcending the ordinary and the mediocre in death, and cultural defeat. Their suicides were testaments to the nobler, higher values of human culture.

Killing oneself for the sake of upholding noble values or for one's ideology and beliefs is no longer considered a heroic act in today's world. Perhaps simply because humanity has lost its nobility of spirit, or perhaps because there are no longer any universal human values considered worthy of sacrificing oneself for. One form of suicide which we did not discuss in the previous chapters is, however, a form of ideological suicide that has been practised for centuries by those who are ready to die and to kill for a cause. Here, it is obviously not the killing of the self which is under question, but the killing of others, because in this case the act of suicide is no longer a personal, individual choice, but rather an ideological imperative for the group. Individuals who have conducted suicide attacks on other individuals, communities or nations throughout history in the name of race, religion, ethnicity or language were known as martyrs, but rarely as men or women who have committed suicide in their own names. For many in different religions, and in secular ideologies like Nazism and fascism, killing oneself in the name of an ideal has been considered an act of self-sacrifice. During the Second World War, the *kamikaze* fighter pilots of the Japanese army were trained as suicide squads. In recent decades, we have seen many acts of suicide bombing by members of the Al-Qaeda and the ISIS, who are trained as *jihadi*s or martyrs for a divine cause in a religious war, and promised glory and immortality in the afterlife. In other words,

> the ideal of martyrdom is constructed in counter-distinction to some real or imagined set of values, in opposition to which martyrdom appears not only desirable but necessary...If living in the shadow of unending war ages you before your time, martyrdom promises eternal youth in a realm where death and the worries and anxieties of the everyday never come to mind. (Edwards 2017: 159–160)

Without doubt, both suicide and martyrdom are voluntary acts, but the practice of killing oneself to attain martyrdom in the service of upholding and preserving an ideology or religion is an act of self-denial where the individual is sacrificed for the cause of the group, while in the case of Seneca, Zweig, Mishima and Celan, suicide is an expression of self-affirmation of the individual. Further, as also shown by different philosophical, ideological and aesthetic approaches to suicide down the ages, the problem of self-destruction is fundamentally linked to the problem of free will and determinism, and the moral rights of individuals versus the moral rights of the society, or God. Therefore, suicide as an individual choice cannot be reduced to a collective phenomenon, unless it is misinterpreted as a form of 'martyrdom' in the name of religion/God, community, nation or the nation-state. In a work interested in understanding the noble essence of suicide, one has to learn to distinguish it from any form of 'voluntary martyrdom'. Interestingly, it is worth noting here that 'there was no Greek or Latin term for a voluntary martyrdom...To be sure, some Roman intellectuals like Celsus characterized Christians as being "out of their mind" for rushing forward to death' (Moss 2012: 539–540).

Let us be clear about one thing: some writers or artists may have thanatophilic tendencies (as is the case with a writer like Mishima), but they rarely embrace death from a necro-political point of view, which justifies and perpetuates martyrdom and its violence against the Otherness of the Other. The central difference between suicide and martyrdom is that the former is an act of self-destruction while the latter is murder, and often mass murder. A suicide bomber, who wants to become a martyr, is someone who gives meaning to his existence not only by dying but also by killing many innocent people. In most cases, suicide bombers kill and die for a religion or an ideology, or just because they are psychopaths. A writer who commits suicide is the sole creator and author of his or her values, purpose and actions. In contrast, revolutions always justify murder, but they never approve of suicides. Unlike revolution, suicide is a claim to absolute freedom. Russian poets like Sergei Esenin or Vladimir Mayakovsky, both of whom committed suicide, had nothing to prove to the Soviet State or its ideology. They remained answerable only to themselves even in the last minutes of their lives.

> Poets who end their lives in...spectacularly well-timed fashion may...be guaranteeing their future immortality. ...Mayakovsky...left behind...a dilemma for a state that found itself faced with the suicide of its best-known artist at a crucial moment in its own self-transformation. [His]...motivations...: were they political, personal, or some unwieldy amalgam of the two? ...Mayakovsky had been killed, the state concluded, by his own lyricism. ...The revolution's bard was dead, shot through the head by a lyrical class enemy who had infiltrated the ranks of the faithful. This was not suicide, in other words, but generic assassination. (Cavanagh 2009: 107)

Here, once again, we are called upon to adopt the logic of suicide as a noble individual act. The one thing we do know is the impossibility of reducing suicide to a rational principle. But the crucial question is whether suicide is a force of life or is it destruction?

If suicide is to remain authentic and noble, it must have a creative role, by giving meaning to the life of the person who has committed suicide and to the lives of others who come after. Where one accepts the concept of suicide, where one confronts it transparently and honestly, one cannot also, without being contradictory, embrace the logic of murder. Why? Because in being fully conscious of the act, the person who commits suicide is well aware of the fact that he or she is giving a meaning to the human life that is left behind. Therefore, suicide creates its own values, which are shared and understood emotionally and rationally by other human beings. It would be wrong to consider suicide as merely disgust or extreme contempt for life. It would be more correct to say that it is a will to judge life freely and to keep within the just bounds of revolt against life's injustices. There is excess in one who enters the omnipotence of death. This hubris would make suicide a revolt against life. Thus, the person who commits suicide is a rebel to life. Yet, in this revolt there is a metaphysical solidarity with all human beings, especially because of the presence of suffering and despair. However, there is no humiliation in a human being who says no to life. Consequently, not every search for new values ends up in suicide, but every act of suicide tacitly invokes a value. This value is not death, but life itself. Suicide proves that it is a movement, a part of life, and that it can only be affirmed by renouncing life. In other words, one could say that, suicide is not an uprooting of life; it is not insensitivity or apathy towards life, but in fact an acknowledgement of its vitality, necessity and inevitability. That is why suicide is perhaps the only form of dying which is beautiful. As Simone Weil argues, 'One thing alone makes the monotony bearable, that is a light from eternity; that is beauty' (Weil 2005: 268). The part of beauty that comes with suicide is eternity.

From the outset, suicide confronts us with the testimony of the eternal man who is grappling with the vicissitudes of time and the condition of evil. The anguish of a modern individual in the face of suicide is that of a person lost in a world without God and without hope. That is why human beings become their own end in the act of suicide. In a world closed to transcendence, the individual finds his or her own mode of transcendence through suicide. The metaphysics of suicide is the cornerstone of unhappiness. Suicide, as the pursuit of unhappiness, questions and challenges the fundamental human values and assumptions of our contemporary society and the ways in which we measure and judge and live life. Reflecting on suicide, its compulsions, doubts, motives and causes, enables us to get a clearer picture of exactly what constitutes unhappiness, and to reflect on its valuable aspects for a meaningful life. For it is only when we know what unhappiness is that we can begin to know happiness. In a world like ours, where happiness and well-being are dictated to us by the State and/or by mass media, culture and shallow, consumerist and ultimately false modes of being, suicide as a mode of unhappiness can be presented as an alternate horizon of truth for human beings.

This, of course, depends on 'if' and 'how' we undertake a critical examination of the concept of 'happiness' in our world. According to Ashis Nandy,

> Perfect happiness comes when one eliminates, one by one, all unhappiness. This is not an easy task. You cannot...eliminate death, old age and...catastrophes. But at least you can live a happy life, the presumption goes...by denying their existence. All societies institutionalise an element of death denial. Only in modern societies does that denial take the form of a panicky repudiation of the idea of death itself. Not only because, in the mythos of modernity, there is no genuine place for the idea of a life after death but also

> because...there is no admission of a natural limit to individual consumption through death. Death denial and a debilitating fear of pain are the obverse of the modern idea of happiness...[which] is consigned... to the domain of the momentary...the mythic or the legendary. (Nandy 2012: 48)

Suicide is a moment of defiance and disobedience of the idea of happiness as a manufactured psychology of contemporary society. For, not to be happy in today's world is, by definition, to be marginal, a misfit and a dissenter. In such a world, unhappiness then becomes the forbidden universe of those who consider suicide to be a singular act of dissent, in contradistinction to the collective normative experience of mediocrity and shallowness. Being exposed to unhappiness, against the authorised context of happiness, is to confront life in its totality, in all its bewildering complexity and beauty.

Suicide is not only something which is 'already there' (*ein Vorhandenes*), but something which is 'its own externality toward itself'. Maybe this is why suicide is inherently unpredictable and disorderly, given the marginality and creativity of those who engage in it. Suicide is a value that falls within a 'common human horizon', since all human beings can understand and commit suicide. Because of this commonality, suicide is morally permissible. This emphasis on the permissibility and possibility of suicide presents itself as a dilemma for an agonistic form of liberalism that avoids taking seriously the permanence of unhappiness in our world. The fact remains that we do live in a world of profound and persistent unhappiness, where the unpleasant and the unacceptable are everyday norms in our social, economic and political structures. We live in a decivilised society with unreal and unrealised hopes. In fact, Stefan Zweig's suicide was a civilisational response to the Nazi decivilising psychology of slaughtering Jews, destroying culture and humanism. And yet, the two definitions of happiness and well-being are built into the mass psychology of our everydayness. This reminds one of the characters of Ray Bradbury's dystopian novel *Fahrenheit 451* who believe that the only way of being happy is by burning books and watching television.

Looking back at the suicides of Zweig, Celan, Mishima, and many other writers, poets, philosophers and artists, one can say that they were all moments of embracing culture against barbarity. For them, the idea and the act of suicide was married to the life of the free mind, and the ethical, aesthetic contemplation of life and death. Through their suicides, they experienced human freedom, art and life. Suicide relieved them of life, without relieving them of living. They wanted to live their lives without being lived by it. If, as Fernando Pessoa says, 'Life is the hesitation between an exclamation and a question' (Pessoa 2015: 315), then to commit suicide is to know when and where to finish a paragraph. Ordinary people hardly understand this. Perhaps because they rarely, if ever, write a paragraph and for them there is little or no difference between an exclamation and a question. The mass of common people are timidly unhappy, but they fear suicide. They live a meaningless existence, but they prefer to be tucked 'into a soft bed of slow death' (Pessoa 2015: 151).

However, the more we live meaningfully, the more we agree with the Czech philosopher Jan Patocka that, 'A life not willing to sacrifice itself to what makes it meaningful is not worth living' (Bažant et al. 2010: 452). What Patocka is pointing at is the essential human desire to preserve one's honour, conscience and dignity in life, through meaningful thought and action. 'When the triumph of evil seems inevitable to men..., there is only one act of liberty left to them, to leave life and thus disclaim any relationship with this evil' (Becker 1975: 257). In other words, suicide is the last Stoic act by which the constructive marginals and dissenters of human civilisation can show that they dominate their human destiny, and are not dominated by it. This freedom of 'coming' and 'going' in life belongs only to outsiders who struggle to preserve their marginality and autonomy in their lives and works. Marginality, it bears repeating, is living on the edge, and not succumbing to the culture of the masses. It suggests an overcoming of the burden of servitude, much as that of old age and physical debilitation. Suicide produces a double shift in the process of everyday life. On the one hand, it fragments the absolute subjectivist ontology, by emerging as a sideline of the rational subject. On the other hand, suicide appears as a broken perception of the world which replaces the linear and monolithic everyday discourse of reality. It is the exit from a world that places the human being under the authority of a closed system of values. Therefore, if suicide is meaningless, then everything is futile and nothing matters. The despotism of God or the State or society pushes the individual to respond to evil with the heroic act of annihilating the self, and to respond to death with death.

Suicide remains the last act of chivalry and integrity in a world of mediocrity and indifference. The writer or the artist who commits suicide repeats the image of the selfless epic knight of yore who excludes all forms of pettiness and calculations in his heroic struggle against the monstrosity of evil and injustice. Paradoxically, the morally courageous act of suicide goes hand in hand with the valourisation of the lost cause that finally asserts itself as the heroism of the writer or artist. This need for the exaltation of moral courage and integrity in the face of tyranny and evil—regardless of its causes and the forms that it takes—and its degrading, dehumanising consequences can only find its final answer in the act of suicide. Seneca saw suicide as the supreme remedy for confronting the tyranny of Nero. Stefan Zweig and Walter Benjamin saw it as the only antidote to the barbarity of the Nazis and the pain and humiliation of exile. It is on the terrain of suicide and the completion of life that the one who takes his or her own life, because of the violence of the world, opens up a new path to immortality—an immortality which is an expression of the experience of the nobility of human spirit. In the light of this nobility of spirit, we can say that on the subject of suicide, a whole family of great minds, from antiquity to modern times, from the East and the West, has thought and pronounced the same judgment: life is a beautiful adventure which deserves to be lived, and lived full and well; but a life in which we do not have an exit door is a solitary confinement. Many philosophers or writers preferred death to such a dishonourable life. However, it would be a grave misunderstanding to consider this will to freedom and autonomy as a form of lunacy or the collapse of reason. Cato and Seneca did not commit suicide because they were madmen, any more than did Celan, Mishimia, Zweig or Benjamin. Ending their lives was for them a way to reassert their authorship over their life and death. As Irina Paperno argues, 'Cato's suicide was associated with freedom—understood as political freedom and personal autonomy—with republicanism, and with dignity—understood as control over one's body and one's emotions' (Paperno, quoted in Marsh 2013: 745).

While it may be naïve to expect a widespread or universal agreement about the ontological and moral status of suicide as a noble and autonomous act signifying the indomitable human will to freedom and immortality, it is undeniable that suicide is a human phenomenon which has existed across time and place since the dawn of human civilisation. The dissent and rebellion associated with the act of suicide comes from the fact that it clearly and categorically raises the question of the relationship between the individual and society. The modernity of suicide also stems from the fact that it poses a fundamental philosophical question about the value of life. If human life is worthwhile and meaningful, then why do human beings turn it into a veritable hell, for themselves and others? Most major religions and modern ideologies have condemned suicide, but they have never been able to find honest and transparent answers to the question of their contribution in making the world a worse, rather than a better, place to live. Perhaps because the majority of religions and ideologies have never been preoccupied with the value of the life of individuals. They do not look directly at either life or death. Suicide, as an anticipation of death, relates directly to life because it determines the ontological and existential value of life. Far from being the opposite of life, suicide invests life with philosophical meaning. It is the awareness of the vital, but mostly lost or forgotten, dimension of life as a mode of creative questioning. From this perspective, suicide no longer designates the nothingness and absurdity of life, but rather its poetic and aesthetic function. In other words, suicide becomes an artist's metaphysics. As Nietzsche observes in *The Birth of Tragedy*: 'we have our highest dignity in our significance as works of art—for it is only as an *aesthetic phenomenon* that existence and the world are eternally *justified*...' (Nietzsche 2000: 52). For Nietzsche, art was a metaphysical consolation. Perhaps we could say the same for suicide. As a transcendental deviation in real life, suicide is a metaphysical consolation. But it is also a necessary path which brings us more fully to the experience of death. In the act of suicide, death is presented as a reality within life. The act of suicide exhorts the human being to recognise his/her individual agency and absolute freedom to transcend life, while also simultaneously affirming that very life.

Nonetheless, either as actors or as spectators of the act of suicide, we in the present day and age cannot but conclude that human life is full of untold suffering and misery and that we are impotent in finding a meaning to this suffering. And further, as science tells us, since there is no life after death, what we are left with is only an endless questioning. Every human being knows that life in general, and more specifically the life of the individual, is not so much an accomplishment as it is a possibility. Truly, suicide then is the end of the present, but it is always a possibility of the future. It is the end for the one who commits suicide, but for those left behind it opens a door to finding the possible meaning of life. As Blaise Pascal says:

> We almost never think of the present, and if we do think of it, it is only to see what light it throws on our plans for the future. The present is never our end. The past and the present are our means, the future alone our end. Thus we never actually live, but hope to live, and since we are always planning how to be happy, it is inevitable that we should never be so. (Pascal 2008: 10)

If the pursuit of unhappiness is a metaphysical dimension of humankind, then suicide is a possible way of transcending the vanity of an indifferent world and reaffirming our humanity.

BIBLIOGRAPHY

Abelsen, Peter. 1996. 'Irony and Purity: Mishima'. *Modern Asian Studies* 30(3), July.

Adorno, Theodor W. 1983. 'Cultural Criticism and Society'. In *Prisms*, 17–34. Cambridge: MIT Press.

———. 2005. *Minima Moralia: Reflections from Damaged Life*. London: Verso.

Alvarez, Alfred. 1971. *The Savage God: A Study of Suicide*. London: Bloomsbury.

Aristotle. 1884. *The Nicomachean Ethics*. Trans. F. H. Peters. London: Kegan Paul.

Balzac, Honoré de. 2012. *The Wild Ass's Skin*. Oxford: Oxford University Press.

Bažant, Jan, Nina Bažantová and Frances Starn. 2010. *The Czech Reader: History, Culture, Politics*. Durham: Duke University Press.

Becker, Lucille. 1975. 'Henry de Montherlant and Suicide'. *Romance Notes* 16(2): 257, Winter.

Beckett, Samuel. 2009. *Three Novels: Molloy, Malone Dies, The Unnameable*. New York: Grove Press.

Berthold, Daniel. 2013. 'Kierkegaard and Camus: Either/Or?'. *International Journal for Philosophy of Religion* 73(2), April.

Brée, Germaine. 1964. *Camus*. Rutgers: Rutgers University Press.

Camus, Albert. 1955. *The Myth of Sisyphus*. Trans. Justin O'Brien. New York: Vintage Books.

———. 1956. *The Rebel*. New York: Vintage Books.

Camus, Albert. 1960. *Resistance, Rebellion and Death*. Trans. Justin O'Brien. New York: Vintage Books.

______. 1975. *The Myth of Sisyphus*. London: Penguin.

______. 2006. *Camus at Combat: Writing 1944–1947*. Ed. Jacqueline Levi-Valensi, Trans. Arthur Goldhammer. Princeton: Princeton University Press.

______. 2017. 'La Crise de l'Homme'. In *Conferences et Discours (1936–1958)*. Paris: Folio-Gallimard.

Cavanagh, Clare. 2009. *Lyric Poetry and Modern Politics: Russia, Poland, and the West*. New Haven: Yale University Press.

Celan, Paul. 1999. *Der Meridian. Endfassung, Vorstufen, Materialien*. Tubinger Ausgabe. Frankfurt/Main: Suhrkamp.

______. 2001. 'In Memoriam Paul Eluard'. In *Selected Poems and Prose of Paul Celan*. New York: Norton.

______. 2002. *Poems of Paul Celan: A Bilingual German/English Edition*. Trans. Michael Hamburger. New York: Persea Books. Revised edition.

______. 2006. 'The Meridian'. In *Paul Celan: Collected Prose*. Trans. Rosemary Waldrop. New York: Routledge.

Cicero. 1927. *Tusculan Disputations*. Trans. J. E. King. London: Heinemann.

Dagan, Hagai. 2001. 'Philosophizing in the Face of Death—Schopenhauer and Rosenzweig'. *Jewish Studies Quarterly* 8(1).

Daviau, Donald G. 1959. 'Stefan Zweig's Victors in Defeat'. *Monatshefte* 51(1), January.

De May, Philippe. 2009. *Lucretius: Poet and Epicurean*. Cambridge: Cambridge University Press.

Donini, Pierluigi. 1999. *The Cambridge History of Hellenistic Philosophy*. Eds. Keimpe Algra, J. Barnes, J. Mansfeld and M. Schofield. Cambridge: Cambridge University Press.

Douglas, Jack D. 1967. *Social Meanings of Suicide*. Princeton: Princeton University Press.

Durkheim, Émile. 1951. *Suicide: A Study in Sociology*. New York: The Free Press.

Edwards, David B. 2017. *Caravan of Martyrs: Sacrifice and Suicide Bombing in Afghanistan*. Berkeley: University of California Press.

Englert, Walter. 1990. 'Seneca and the Stoic View of Suicide'. *The Society for Ancient Greek Philosophy Newsletter* 184.

Eshel, Amir. 2004. 'Paul Celan's Other: History, Poetics, and Ethics'. *New German Critique* 91, Special Issue on Paul Celan, Winter.

Felstiner, John. 1982. 'Translating Celan's Last Poem'. *The American Poetry Review* 11(4), July/August.

———. 2001. *Paul Celan: Poet, Survivor, Jew*. New Haven: Yale University Press.

———. 2004. 'Paul Celan Meets Samuel Beckett'. *The American Poetry Review* 33(4), July/August.

Funatsu, Yasushi. 2001. 'Britain Feared a Revival of Militarism after Mishima's Suicide'. *The Japan Times*. 3 January. Available at https://www.japantimes.co.jp/news/2001/01/03/national/britain-feared-a-revival-of-militarism-after-mishimas-suicide/#.XsuJWmgzbIV (accessed September 2020).

Garrison, Elise P. 1991. 'Attitudes toward Suicide in Ancient Greece'. *Transactions of the American Philological Association (1974–2014)* 121.

Gillespie, John K. 1982. 'Beyond Byzantium: Aesthetic Pessimism in Mishima's Modern Noh Plays'. *Monumenta Nipponica* 37(1), Spring.

Gordon, Daniel. 2016. 'From Act to Fact: The Transformation of Suicide in Western Thought'. *Historical Reflections /Réflexions Historiques* 42(2), Summer.

Graham, Daniel W. 2016. 'Socrates' Mission'. *BYU Studies Quarterly* 55(4).

Gupta, Anoop. 2005. *Kierkegaard's Romantic Legacy: Two Theories of the Self*. Ottawa: University of Ottawa Press.

Hecht, Jennifer Michael. 2013. *Stay: A History of Suicide and the Philosophies Against It*. New Haven: Yale University Press.

Hubbard, Ben. 2016. *Samurai Warriors*. London: Cavendish Square Publishing.

Hume, David. 2006. *Moral Philosophy*. Ed. Geoffrey Sayre-McCord. Indianapolis: Hackett Publishing.

Ilg, Ulrike. 2002. 'Painted Theory of Art: "Le Suicidé" (1877) by Édouard Manet and the Disappearance of Narration'. *Artibus et Historiae* 23(45).

Kant, Immanuel. 1964a. *Groundwork of the Metaphysic of Morals*. Trans. H. Paton. New York: Harper & Row.

______. 1964b. *Metaphysical Principles of Virtue*. Trans. J. Ellington. Indianapolis: Bobbs-Merrill.

Kierkegaard, Søren. 1987. *Either/Or*, Vol. 1. Eds. and trans. Howard V. Hong and Edna H. Hong. Princeton: Princeton University Press.

______. 1990. *Eighteen Upbuilding Discourses*. Eds. and trans. Howard V. Hong and Edna H. Hong. Princeton: Princeton University Press.

______. 1993. *Three Discourses on Imagined Occasions*. Eds. and trans. Howard V. Hong and Edna H. Hong. Princeton: Princeton University Press.

______. 2009. *The Portable Kierkegaard*. Ed. Simon Yee. Canada: Vintage Books.

Klink, Joanna. 2000. 'You: An Introduction to Paul Celan'. *The Iowa Review* 30(1), Spring–Summer.

Langley, Eric. 2009. *Narcissism and Suicide in Shakespeare and His Contemporaries*. Oxford: Oxford University Press.

Long, A. A. 1988. 'Socrates in Hellenistic Philosophy'. *The Classical Quarterly* 38(1).

Madame de Staël. 1813. *The Influence of the Passions Upon the Happiness of Individuals and of Nations*. London: Henry Colburn.

______. 1816. *Reflections on Suicide*. Philadelphia: Edward Earle, J. Maxwell, Printer.

Mann, Thomas. 1963. *Briefe 1937–1947*. Ed. Erika Mann. Frankfurt/Main: S. Fischer.

Marmysz, John. 2017. *Cinematic Nihilism: Encounters, Confrontations, Overcomings*. Edinburgh: Edinburgh University Press.

Marsh, Ian. 2013. 'The Uses of History in the Unmaking of Modern Suicide'. *Journal of Social History* 46(3), Spring. *The Politics of Suicide: Historical Perspectives on Suicidology before Durkheim*.

Melanowicz, Mikolaj. 1992. 'The Power of Illusion: Mishima Yukio and "Madame de Sade"'. *Japan Review* 3: 6.

Michaux, Henri. 1997. *Darkness Moves: An Henri Michaux Anthology, 1927–1984*. Berkeley: University of California Press.

Merrill, Kenneth R. 1999. 'Hume on Suicide'. *History of Philosophy Quarterly* 16(4), October.

Miles, Murray. 2001. 'Plato on Suicide ("Phaedo" 60C–63C)'. *Phoenix* 55(3/4), Autumn–Winter.

Montaigne, Michel de. 1965. *The Complete Essays*. Palo Alto: Stanford University Press.

Mishima, Yukio. 1963. *Confessions of a Mask*. Trans. Meredith Weatherby. New York: New Directions.

______. 1966. 'Patriotism'. In *Death in Midsummer and other Stories*. New York: New Directions.

______. 1970a. *Sun and Steel*. Trans. John Bester. Tokyo, London: Kodansha International.

______. 1970b. *Sun and Steel*. New York: Grove Press.

______. 1979. *Yukio Mishima on Hagakure: The Samurai Ethic and Modern Japan*. London: Penguin Books.

Morrison, Ken. 1998. 'Durkheim and Schopenhauer: New Textual Evidence on the Conceptual History of Durkheim's Formulation of the Egoistical Truistic Types of Suicide'. *Durkheimian Studies /Études Durkheimiennes*, New Series, Vol. 4.

Moss, Candida R. 2012. 'The Discourse of Voluntary Martyrdom: Ancient and Modern'. *Church History* 81(3), September.

Müller-Sievers, Helmut. 2004. 'On the Way to Quotation: Paul Celan's "Meridian" Speech'. *New German Critique* 91: 146, Special Issue on Paul Celan, Winter.

Nandy, Ashis. 2012. 'The Idea of Happiness'. *Economic and Political Weekly* 47(2): 48, 14 January.

Nathan, John. 1975. *Mishima: A Biography*. Boston: Little, Brown and Company.

Nemoto, Reiko Tachiban. 1993. 'The Obsession to Destroy Monuments: Mishima and Böll'. *Twentieth Century Literature* 39(2), Summer.

Nietzsche, Friedrich. 2000. *Beyond Good and Evil*. In *Basic Writings of Nietzsche*. Trans. and ed. Walter Kaufmann. New York: The Modern Library.

Noon, Georgia. 1978. 'On Suicide'. *Journal of the History of Ideas* 39(3), July–September.

Paperno, Irina. 2013. 'Suicide as a Cultural Institution in Dostoevsky's Russia', 10note6, quoted in Ian Marsh, 2013, 'The Uses of History in the Unmaking of Modern Suicide', *Journal of Social History* 46(3): 745, 'The Politics of Suicide: Historical Perspectives on Suicidology before Durkheim' (Spring 2013).

Pascal, Blaise. 2008. *Human Happiness*. London: Penguin Books.

Pessoa, Fernando. 2015. *The Book of Disquiet*. London: Penguin Classics.

Plato. 1997. *Complete Works*. Ed. John M. Cooper. Indianapolis: Hackett Publishing.

Prater, Donald A. 1972. *European of Yesterday: A Biography of Stefan Zweig*. Oxford: Clarendon Press.

______. 1982. 'Stefan Zweig'. In *Exile: The Writer's Experience*. Eds. John M. Spalek and Robert F. Bell. Chapel Hill: University of North Carolina Press.

Prochnik, George. 2017. 'When It's Too Late to Stop Fascism, According to Stefan Zweig'. *The New Yorker*, 6 February.

Reale, Giovanni. 1985. *A History of Ancient Philosophy III: The Systems of the Hellenistic Age*. Albany: SUNY Press.

Ross, Christopher. 2006. *Mishima's Sword: Travels in Search of a Samurai Legend*. Sydney: Harper Perennial.

Sacharoff, Mark. 1972. 'Suicide and Brutus' Philosophy in Julius Caesar'. *Journal of the History of Ideas* 33(1), January–March.

Saint Augustine of Hippo. 2015. *The City of God*. Altenmunster: Jazzybee Verlag.

______. 2012–2017. *City of God* (De Citate Dei), Books I–XI. New Apostolic Bible Covenant.

Sanderson, Richard K. 1992. 'Suicide as Message and Metadrama in English Renaissance Tragedy'. *Comparative Drama* 26(3), Fall.

Sartre, J. P. 1956. *Being and Nothingness*. New York: Washington Square Press.

Schopenhauer, Arthur. 1964. *The World as Will and Idea*, Vol. 3. London: Routledge.

______. 1970. *Essays and Aphorisms*. New York: Penguin Classics.

______. 1974. *Parega and Paralipomena*. Trans. E. Payne. Oxford: Clarendon Press.

Scott-Stokes, Henry. 1974. *The Life and Death of Yukio Mishima*. New York: Farrar, Straus and Giroux.

Seidler, Michael J. 1983. 'Kant and the Stoics on Suicide'. *Journal of the History of Ideas* 44(3), July–September.

Seneca. 1928. *On Anger*, Book III, 15.4. In *Moral Essays*, Vol. 1. Trans. John W. Basore. London: W. Heinemann.

______. 1997. *On the Shortness of Life*. London: Penguin Books.

______. 2016a. *Epistle* 58 (32–34). In *Seneca Six Pack*. Los Angeles: Enhanced Media.

______. 2016b. *Letters from a Stoic*, Vol. 1. Los Angeles: Enhanced Media.

______. 2016c. *Seneca's Letters from a Stoic*. New York: Dover Publications.

______. 2017. *Letters from a Stoic*, Letter LXX. In *Seneca Six Pack 2: Six More Essential Texts*. Los Angeles: Enhanced Media.

______. 2018. *How to Die: An Ancient Guide to the End of Life*. Princeton: Princeton University Press.

Shakespeare, William. 1770. *The Life and Death of King Richard II*. London: A. Donaldson.

______. 1836. *The Works of Shakespeare*. London: Isaac, Tuckey and Co.

Sherif, Ann. 2003. 'Mishima Yukio'. In *The Columbia Companion to Modern East Asian Literature*, eds. Joshua S. Mostow, Kirk A. Denton, Bruce Fulton and Sharalyn Orbaugh. New York: Columbia University Press.

Slights, Camille Wells. 1981. *The Casuistical Tradition in Shakespeare, Donne, Herbert, and Milton*, Princeton: Princeton University Press.

Smith, Steven B. 2012. *Political Philosophy*. New Haven: Yale University Press.

Stern, Howard. 1983. 'Verbal Mimesis: The Case of "Die Winzer"'. *Studies in 20th Century Literature* 8(1): 23–39.

Steiner, George. 2011. *The Poetry of Thought: From Hellenism to Celan*. New York: A New Directions Book.

Steiner, George and Laure Adler. 2017. *A Long Saturday: Conversations*. Chicago: The University of Chicago Press.

Stuckenschmidt, H. H. 2011. *Schoenberg: His Life, World and Works*. Trans. Humphrey Searle. Surrey: Oneworld Classics.

Suied, Alain. 1999. 'Paul Celan: Poet of the Shoah'. *New Literary History* 30(1), Poetry & Poetics, Winter.

Wallace, John R. 1997. 'Tarrying with the Negative: Aesthetic Vision in Murasaki and Mishima'. *Monumenta Nipponica* 52(2): 181–199, Summer.

Warren, James. 2001. 'Socratic Suicide'. *The Journal of Hellenic Studies* 121: 91–106.

Weil, Simone. 2005. *An Anthology*. London: Penguin Classics.

Wolfe, Alan Stephen. 2014. *Suicidal Narrative in Modern Japan: The Case of Dazai Osamu*. Princeton: Princeton University Press.

Yamanouchi, Hisaaki. 1972. 'Mishima Yukio and His Suicide'. *Modern Asian Studies* 6(1): 1–16, January.

Yourcenar, Margarite. 1986. 'Mishima: A Vision of the Void'. *The New York Times Book Review*, 2 November, Section 7.

Zweig, Stefan. 1942. 'Zweig's Suicide Letter'. 22 February. Zweig's Papers at the National Library of Israel (NLI). Petropolis. Available at: https://gizra.github.io/CDL/pages/4FB68FFB-D884-EE6A-4A8B-2AF40CD10E3B/ (accessed September 2020).

______. 1943. *The World of Yesterday*. London: Cassell.